BLACK STAR

OTHER BOOKS ABOUT AFRICA
BY BASIL DAVIDSON

History

Old Africa Rediscovered
Black Mother: The African Slave Trade
The African Past: Chronicles from Antiquity to Modern Times
The Africans: An Entry to Cultural History
Africa in History: Themes and Outlines
A History of West Africa AD 1000–1800 with J. A. Ade Ajayi
and F. K. Bush
A History of East and Central Africa to the Late 19th Century
with J. E. F. Mhina
African Kingdoms with the Editors of Time-Life Books
Guide to African History
Discovering Our African Heritage

Contemporary Affairs

Report on Southern Africa
The New West Africa: Symposium ed. with A. Ademola
The African Awakening
Which Way Africa? The Search for a New Society
The Liberation of Guiné: Aspects of an African Revolution
In the Eye of the Storm: Angola's People

Fiction

The Rapids

Basil Davidson

BLACK STAR

A View of the Life and Times of
Kwame Nkrumah

PRAEGER PUBLISHERS

New York · Washington

Published in the United States of America in 1974
by Praeger Publishers, Inc.
111 Fourth Avenue, New York, N.Y. 10003

Library of Congress Cataloging in Publication Data

Davidson, Basil, 1914–
    Black Star; a view of the life and times of Kwame
Nkrumah.

    1. Nkrumah, Kwame, Pres. Ghana, 1909–1972.
I. Title.
DT512.3.N57D38   966.7'05'0924 [B]   73–16035

Printed in Great Britain

Contents

Acknowledgements

I wish to thank many for their comments in conversation or in correspondence, at one point or another, on the problems of taking a balanced view of the life and times of Kwame Nkrumah; and especially Sir Alfred Ayer, Djibo Bakary, Vasco Cabral, Michael Dei-Anang, Abdoulaye Diallou, Christopher Fyfe and the Centre of African Studies at the University of Edinburgh, Thomas Hodgkin, Alhajji Babatunde Jose, Kenneth King, Julian Rea, David Williams, and Jack Woddis; none of them, I must emphasize, is responsible for any myopia there may be in the view taken here. My constant debt to the recording virtues of *West Africa* and to its distinguished editor, will be obvious to readers.

I am grateful to the following people for permission to use material: C. Fyfe, G. Bing, W. Scott-Thompson, D. Austin, M. Dei-Anang and the Institute of Commonwealth Relations, and Panaf Books Ltd, 243 Regent Street, London, W1R 8PN for material from *An Autobiography of Kwame Nkrumah*, first published in 1957.

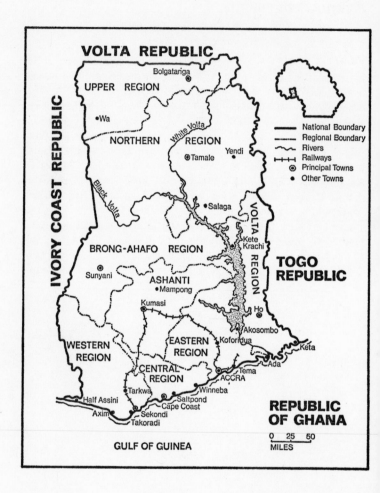

VOLTA REPUBLIC

UPPER REGION

Bolgatanga

•Wa

NORTHERN REGION

White Volta

◉Tamale   Yendi

Black Volta

•Salaga

BRONG-AHAFO REGION

Kete Krachi

VOLTA REGION

Sunyani

TOGO REPUBLIC

ASHANTI
•Mampong

Kumasi

Ho

Akosombo

EASTERN REGION

Koforidua

Keta

Ada

WESTERN REGION

CENTRAL REGION

Tema

ACCRA

Winneba

Tarkwa

Saltpond
Cape Coast

Half Assini

Axim

Sekondi
Takoradi

IVORY COAST REPUBLIC

REPUBLIC OF GHANA

GULF OF GUINEA

——	National Boundary
─·─·─	Regional Boundary
∿∿	Rivers
┼┼┼	Railways
◉	Principal Towns
•	Other Towns

0   25   50
MILES

Prologue

The Man on the Steamer Deck

Speak of me as I am; nothing extenuate,
Nor set down aught in malice.

Othello

During old colonial times, the years that Amilcar Cabral has termed the period of classical colonialism, travellers between Europe and Africa went by sea because travel by air was impossible or still a rare adventure.

In November 1947, rather more than two years after the second world war, the motorship *Accra* cleared the port of Liverpool on a grey winter's day like any other. As she set her bows to the winds of the Irish Channel, turning south for the Atlantic, her voyage appeared in no way different in its meaning from all the countless colonial sailings of the West African run. Yet there was a difference, even a large one. If only two men noticed it at the time, history would repair the error.

This difference consisted in a couple of obscure passengers bound for the Gold Coast, the colonial name of Ghana, one of England's oldest African colonies. To these men, at least, this voyage of the *Accra* had a singular meaning. They were going home; beyond that, though, one of them was going with a mission to lead his country to independence, and his companion meant to participate in that difficult and risky enterprise. As Kwame Nkrumah and Kojo Botsio watched the shores of England fade along the skylines of November, they knew that, one way or the other, nothing would be the same again.

The *Accra* went on its way, and no one bothered these two passengers. There had been a little trouble with the police before embarking at Liverpool, for Nkrumah had acquired a very radical reputation with the British authorities, partly by associating with well-known trouble-makers such as the Kenyan agitator, Jomo Kenyatta, and partly by reason of his own speeches and activities. He could expect trouble when he got home at last, for the colonial authorities would be well informed of the contents of his 'police file' in England, or at least of what the British police thought those contents meant. The colonial authorities would be waiting to follow quietly on his trail; or, if necessary, not quietly. But meanwhile the voyage proceeded without incident.

And that, too, was not in the least strange. Generations of Africans had sailed this way, returning home from a visit to the 'imperial mother' and her sacred shrines. Some had travelled from curiosity; others for business; most for the advancement of their careers. They would come back home again with the prestige attaching to 'been to's', and stand a better chance of rising in the scale of colonial society. If they had picked up any dangerous thoughts in Europe, they would soon forget them; if they didn't forget them, the authorities would quickly help them to a safer state of mind. Such examples were known; but Nkrumah and Botsio, two studious men keeping themselves studiously apart, could in any case have seemed no different from all the others.

Besides, who could really think that a mission to win African independence was good for more than a laugh? Round the long reach of the West African seaboard, running far to the south-ward and then to the east, the *Accra* and her passengers coasted past the shores of one colony after another. In none of these colonies did the rulers have the smallest doubt, in those years, that their rule would continue for many and even uncountable years into the future. They thought this obvious, and they were sure that it was right. Having emerged from the war against Hitler's Germany and Mussolini's Italy, the great European empires in Africa seemed by all outward appearances to stand perfectly intact, immensely strong, untouchable.

There might be a few people who thought differently, but the colonial powers would deal with them according to their rules.

In all these colonies without exception, whether French or Spanish, British or Portuguese, the rulers were routinely on the trail of people like Nkrumah, or, whenever they preferred it, had shut the doors of prison cells on such undesirable or crazy persons. Nkrumah was soon going to share in the experience.

His immediate plan was to arrange a conference of nationalists from all the British West African colonies, and, if possible, from other colonies as well. Nothing was to come of this; but it steered his route upon this journey home. He had meant to land at Bathurst in the Gambia, but the *Accra* had no business there and sailed on to Freetown in Sierra Leone. There Nkrumah took leave of Botsio and went ashore.

He spent two busy weeks in Freetown where he discussed his plans with the veteran anti-colonialist Wallace Johnson and with others, and also spoke at several public meetings. Then he continued to Monrovia in Liberia. Could Liberia join such a conference? Its spokesmen thought this more than doubtful. Liberia, they told Nkrumah, was already an independent country. Somewhat depressed by this reception, the traveller again took ship for Takoradi, the Gold Coast's only deep-water harbour.

This time he travelled less comfortably. Having in mind what the police files might contain, what almost certainly they must contain, he travelled discreetly. As a deck passenger he could keep his name to himself, the sole and meagre privilege that deck passengers enjoy, but in this case a useful one. The question now was not so much whether the Gold Coast authorities would allow him ashore, for they were practically bound to do this, since he was born and bred a native of the country. The real question was whether they would allow him ashore in liberty. He thought it far from certain. Wouldn't they prefer to find some excuse for holding him in prison—all that talk of 'communism' in the files—while looking for another excuse to deport him?

It is not much distance from Monrovia to Takoradi. For Nkrumah, leaning on the rail with such thoughts in mind, there was the long low headland of Cape Palmas, famous landmark in the old days of the sailing ships, the old days of the slave trade; and then, not much beyond, the outline of the lagoons and shoreland of the Ivory Coast with a few lamps winking yellowly at night. There too, in 1947, African nationalists were to be found; and some were not in prison. One or two were even members of the newly-reconstructed French National Assembly in Paris. Nkrumah had lately gone to France to see them, and had concluded that they were going to have no easy time of it. The omens for himself were certainly no better.

Yet everything began easily. As so often in his life, then and later, the hardest tests did not come at the beginning. He went ashore at Takoradi; and it was all quite easy. He stood in the queue and handed his passport to an African immigration officer. This man read his name and paused, then grinned and pulled the traveller aside. 'He shook my hand enthusiastically,' the traveller afterwards recalled. And the same man explained to Nkrumah that a lot of people were waiting eagerly for his return. He went on through customs, and found some of his friends. The next day he left Takoradi for his own district, in the far south-west, where his mother lived. His mission could begin.

Within a little more than three years he had given his leadership to a complete change in the situation. At the outset of 1951 he emerged from prison to become Leader of Government Business in a cabinet dominated by Africans, and then Prime Minister of the Gold Coast, the first of all the colonies of black Africa south of the Sahara to exercise the right of internal self-rule. Within less than ten years he carried the Gold Coast to full political independence, once more leading the way for the rest of black Africa.

Everywhere in these vast tropical regions the black star of Ghana's independence became a symbol of hope and resurgence. For colony after colony, far even into the dim obscurities of the Belgian Congo or the silence of the colonies of Portugal, Nkrumah's name and significance signalled the beginning of a new life. Across the world it gave black people a claim to dignity and self-respect of a kind that they had not known for generations. It challenged the myths of black inferiority, servitude, backwardness.

Much later again, long after this man had been driven into exile, the magic of his work still held firm among a great many people in many lands. If he was allowed home again only after death, it was even so to receive the highest funeral honours that Ghana could bestow. The village of his birth and burial, Nkroful, became a place of pilgrimage.

*

Nkrumah's return in 1947 marked the opening of a new era. Even his most severe critics have not thought this claim to be excessive: 'To the black man in all parts of the world Nkrumah gave a new pride.'* His admirers have thought it certain: 'He was above all,' Cabral has said, 'the strategist of genius in the struggle against classical colonialism.'

History will therefore have much to say about Nkrumah in the calm judgement of the future: it will place him at the heart and centre of the whole great process of primary decolonization. But today, looking at his life and work, one has to find a path to truth through all the blame and praise that followed in his wake; and it is not easy to find this path. The fact is that no final judgement is possible as yet; and a full biography of Nkrumah cannot be sensibly attempted at this time.

What follows here is an attempt to show and to explain him in the framework of his times, an effort at comprehension that other historians, better instructed in the future, may correct or improve. To some extent, necessarily, it is a personal memoir, for I knew him fairly well through many of those years, beginning in my own case in 1952; but I have tried to balance my own opinions against those of others, for or against, and to tell this story 'as it was'.

Public figures who challenge the established order of their times, and who go on doing this even when their first aims are achieved, must fear adulation and expect abuse. Did Nkrumah

* Editorial in *The Legon Observer*, Legon, Ghana, 18 May 1972.

receive more of the first than he desired, or more of the second than he deserved? Such questions will long be open to debate. What now seems obvious is that a final judgement will reject those who have seen him as a devil, as well as those who have seen him as a superman. For a final judgement will weigh merits against defects, successes against failures; and with Nkrumah there was always plenty of all of these. Their abundance was precisely what gave his life and work their drama, and their strong emotive force.

Part of the difficulty in telling a balanced story, in reaching what history will accept as truth, comes from this abundance. Another part of the difficulty comes from the sheer extremeness of contrary opinions about him. If many of these opinions have 'something in them', how much do they have; and which, on balance, is nearer to the facts? The same critics who praised him for giving black people everywhere a new pride in themselves also denounced him as 'vain, corrupt, and tyrannical', and his regime as 'monstrous, tyrannical and oppressive personal rule'.*
Those of a different view may think of such critics as mere observers standing on the sidelines. Yet it remains that no leader who evokes such bitterness among honest if prejudiced observers can escape some responsibility for the strength and persistence of their opinions.

Many who knew him well found him a different person from the devil of his detractors, just as they also found him different from the godlike hero of his praise-singers. Their evidence points rather to someone who, at least in everyday life, held a firm grip on the perils of political power, and who, at least till near the end, distrusted the vanities of power as well. They speak rather of a man whose personal life was simple and even unassuming, full of humour, closely dependent upon those he loved or liked, and devoted with a rare excellence of purpose to the causes in which he believed. These witnesses, too, must have some truth upon their side.

His weaknesses were never in much doubt. He was a man of

* A. A. Boahen, *The Legon Observer*, 8 November 1972, pp. 24, 21.

soaring vision more often than of calculating thought. This vision could obscure his understanding of what was possible and what was not. He was an insistent optimist; this optimism could mislead him badly. Though he believed firmly in organization, he had little patience with humdrum detail, was quickly bored by routine, and preferred to contemplate the distant summits of his vision rather than inspect the immediate soil beneath his feet. He made great things happen. But he was not, in any ordinary sense, a clever politician. In quite a large sense, he was not a politician at all.

The contradiction in his character took many forms; perhaps it does so in every person of outstanding talent and great purpose. He was first and foremost a man of ideas; and yet he was forced throughout his active life to behave as a man of action. He wanted above all to make life better for ordinary people; yet because of his long absence in America, and then in England, he had little knowledge of the practical realities of life for ordinary people. His vision called for nothing less than a revolution that should lead to socialism and unite a continent; but he came to power in a colony where a gentle process of reform was accepted by nearly all his fellow-countrymen as being quite enough.

It is easy to list his weaknesses. Yet they do not emerge, one may repeat, as being of the nature that his most vocal enemies have liked to describe. They do not appear as the faults of a man of violence and hatred. One of his critics, a European long employed at a university which Nkrumah greatly helped to build, has likened his rule in Ghana to Hitler's in Germany. Even an interim judgement will find any such comparison absurd. Nkrumah and Hitler had nothing in common. Many of his enemies were to have good reason to be thankful for the fact.

He aroused irritation and anger outside Africa, especially in the old imperial countries. It is easy to see why, though sometimes hard to understand why such feelings were expressed with so much vehemence and malice. He greatly speeded up the whole process of political decolonization, not only in Ghana but widely elsewhere; later, he began to tackle the problems of economic decolonization, and trod again on many greatly self-respecting toes. He spoke for black equality as though it were a right which needed no discussion. He took for granted what the white man's world wished to concede as a gift, expecting gratitude; yet he was not thankful. There were many who came to accept what he had done, but not to forgive him for it.

He had African critics from the first; some became his most bitter enemies, and this was seldom his fault. Unless he had surrendered all his plans and convictions, it could not have been otherwise. Later, he made critics among other Africans; often, with these, the fault was on his side. This was also true of Africans outside Ghana. Some rejected the flamboyance of his style. Others rejected his interference.

His work remains: in its essentials, beyond any doubt, a major work for Africa's progress. History will dissect his failings with a dry and careful hand. But it will measure these against his achievements, judging him always as a leader who was bound to act within his own capacities, and within the possibilities of his time. This will be the background of reality, of the choices that were really there, of the options that were really open, against which history will answer our questions, and will seat him in its pantheon. Meanwhile, what happened?

*

Travelling home discreetly from Monrovia to Takoradi, all those years ago, the man on the steamer's deck may have had some notion of what the future could have in store. Yet it seems more likely, as will appear in due course, that his only certainty was that the future was going to be difficult, and would try him hard.

For the moment, he went happily ashore and found his friends and telephoned to others, rejoicing at being safely home, and then went off to see his mother. His mother had said farewell to him twelve years earlier. Now she failed in the first moments to recognize her son for who he was and what he had become.

Others, for other reasons, were about to make the same mistake.

1. Dreams and Visions

I was made aware that here was no ordinary teacher.
The Rev. Wynne Jones, Gold Coast Schools Inspector,
writing of 1932

HOW HE BEGAN

Nkrumah was born to the senior wife of a goldsmith of the
Nzima language-group who live in the south-western corner of
Ghana: probably, he himself thought, on a Saturday in mid-
September of the year 1909.

His mother used to say that the true date was 1912, but a
Roman Catholic priest who baptized the young Nkrumah wrote
1909 in his records, and that seems to be the right date. He was
a village boy close to the customs of his people, the child of a
large and easy-going family. This family was part of a people
who have lived since time immemorial in sound of the sea, who
knew in their time the first small ships from Europe, and who
have played a vivid role in the commercial life of their coastland:
an out-going, self-confident, hard-working sort of people,
accustomed more than most peoples to the chances and changes
of life.

He will have listened when a boy to many tales of distant
venturing and travel by sea or land. That was to be important
for him, and all the more, perhaps, because he was a shy child
who preferred to stand and listen to his elders rather than
merely run with the crowd. He sucked in knowledge of the
challenges of life, and dreamed dreams about the power a man
can have to meet and overcome them. It was a habit of mind
that stayed with him, a counterpart to his horror of violence and
his later admiration for Gandhi and the pacifism which Gandhi
preached.

His mother meant much to him. A strong-minded woman, she made sure that he went to school, and remained a central figure to him throughout his life. It was characteristic of the grown man that she should be the first person whom he sought when returning from his years abroad. Perhaps it was also for this reason, this importance to him of his mother, that he never found it easy to make a close and lasting relationship with any other woman. He used to say that women frightened him, explaining in 1957, when he was nearly fifty, that 'it is not fear today, but something deeper. Perhaps it is a dread of being trapped, of being in some way overpowered.'

There would be several women in his life to whom he gave his confidence. But the evidence suggests that he preferred to keep the relationship informal, although his one marriage, embarked on late in life, seems to have brought him happiness as well as a good wife and children. He had a large need for love and affection, and was capable of showing both. But it is also true that he showed these feelings with reserve, and this reserve was to be an obstacle to the confidence that others might wish to give him in return.

How soon he really felt himself to be somehow 'set apart', and bound to the fulfilment of a mission, is another matter. In any political sense, that came much later. Yet the fact remains that he was set apart as early as the age of nine from the great majority of boys and girls in the Gold Coast of his youth. The elementary school of Half Assini was no great academy, yet only a few children crossed its portals then. And of those few, fewer still stayed beyond the first year, the so-called 'infant year'. Gold Coast records for 1911 show that 10,874 children were enrolled in the 'infant year' at the colony's schools, but only 2,057 were in Standard 1, and no more than 387 in Standard 7, the final year of elementary schooling. The situation was still about the same when Nkrumah began his own 'infant year'.

He completed all seven standards, in itself something special in those times. And then, setting him apart once again, he went on to become a pupil-teacher. He had not only done well at his books and games; he had also showed a rare determination and self-discipline. No 'colonial child' could hope to stay the full elementary course, and then raise himself into teacher's rank, without powerful qualities of brain and character. Even in the Gold Coast, an 'advanced colony' as things went in those days, a child of humble parents had to be an outstanding child if he or she were going to win any of the prizes offered by education.

This was not because of any lack of bright children, or because these children did not want to go to school. On the contrary, those were years of tremendous educational demand. The schools were besieged for places. 'Never in the course of my experience of the tropics,' a British governor of the Gold Coast said in 1919, 'have I found a place where the people were so avid for education. It is the only country, I fancy, where the schoolboy, without being a prig, is more anxious to go to school than his parents are to send him.'

Yet there were few schools, few places in the schools, and few parents able and willing to meet the cost of keeping their children at their books. Nkrumah had brains and grit. But he had the chance, too, of going to school and staying there. He was also born at a lucky time for go-ahead young men in the Gold Coast; and it is useful to see why. For the answer explains a great deal about the later life and development of this earnest young teacher in the elementary school at Half Assini.

EARLY ENTERPRISES

His first big chance came in 1926. It was to open the door to all that followed, and he seized it with joy, though also with an understandable fear that he might not be able to meet its difficult challenge.

In 1926 he had begun to teach in the small town of Half Assini, and might have so continued for the rest of his working life. There were only a handful of secondary schools in the country, and Nkrumah lacked in any case the necessary education for teaching in them. And in those days there were no worth-while jobs for a teacher save in teaching.

But in 1919 there had come to the Gold Coast, as Britain's governor, a man who already knew the country and respected its people. This governor, Gordon Guggisberg, was one who greatly believed in the 'imperial mother's' mission to help the Africans. It is possible to judge him simply as a clever paternalist who wanted to improve the colonial system so as to make it stronger; but that would be to judge him outside the context of his times. Guggisberg thought the colonial system the only possible system there could be; but he also thought that in the end the Africans would take it over and work it for themselves.

That was an old British tradition in West Africa. As long before as 1853 a British minister, Lord Grey, had put it into words. 'The true policy I believe to be,' he said, 'the formation of a regular government on the European model, so that the interference of the British authorities may be less and less required.' Nowadays this policy might be called 'neo-colonialism'. In Guggisberg's day, more than half a century ago, it was thought enlightened; in a colonial sense, it was enlightened. Guggisberg set out to follow it.

This kind of colonial governor was less rare in British West Africa than elsewhere in the dispossessed continent. One reason why was that there were no white settlers in the British West African colonies. Even the big trading companies owned very little land, or none at all. Several of them had tried to get hold of land, but they had met with strong African opposition, and, because there were no white farming settlers, they had failed. Besides this, Britain had occupied these colonies partly by alliance with local peoples, and these local peoples had struggled for their rights. So it was accepted, at least in principle, that 'in the end' the Africans would recover their independence. Guggisberg thought it his duty to make 'the end' somewhat less remote in time.

He became Governor with two ideas in mind. He wanted more economic enterprise and tried to promote it, rightly seeing that

Ghana's 'one crop economy'—its reliance on cocoa exports—was bad for the country. Secondly, he wanted more education for Africans, and in this he had some success. He spurred on the opening of new schools, gave teachers some improvement in their very low wages, and set about raising the standard of teaching. Much came out of this. In 1924 there was established at Achimota, not far from the capital of Accra, the colony's first high-quality training college for teachers.

The principal of this new college, the Rev. A. G. Fraser, was allowed to select his own staff; and Fraser chose for his vice-principal a man whose name is still honoured in Ghana, and likely long to remain so. This was Kwegyir Aggrey, a Gold Coaster from the seaboard country who had spent twenty-two years in the United States, teaching and studying, and who now returned with the aim of providing, at Achimota, an education that would be fully worthy of world citizenship. Though Aggrey died in 1927, his vigour and ideals achieved great things at Achimota. The 'winds of all the world' began to blow through its classrooms. The lessons of Black America as well of white America became a stimulus and challenge.

Fraser and Aggrey set out to look for promising students, encouraged by Guggisberg who shared their belief that stores of talent lay hidden in the schools. One day in 1926 Fraser went down to Half Assini. He listened to the lessons given by Half Assini's teachers, and put in a recommendation that Kwame Nkrumah, then aged seventeen, should be admitted to Achimota.

Nkrumah stayed at Achimota for four years. After that he taught as a head or senior teacher in schools more advanced than Half Assini's. How well he taught was still vividly remembered forty years later by a former schools inspector, the Rev. Wynne Jones. He recalled in a letter to the *Sunday Telegraph* of 6 August, 1972, going to inspect a Roman Catholic junior school where Nkrumah was teaching 'in the local Fanti dialect'.

'I have never forgotten our meeting,' he wrote from his retirement in Wales, 'since I was suddenly made aware that here was no ordinary teacher. Despite a frieze of noisy spectators at the open windows, the pupils reacted to his calm, dignified and 'magnetic' manner whole-heartedly. It was an unforgettable inspectorial experience.'

Achimota had opened windows on the world for Nkrumah. Working at his own development, he eventually decided to visit the United States. That was when the major chapters of his life began for him. The years that he spent in the United States became his formative period. As they shaped him, so later did he think and behave in the years of his political leadership.

What ideas did he take with him there? How did he then see the future: his own, but also his country's and Africa's?

*

Now that most of Africa is politically independent, and other obstacles stand in the way of progress, it is not easy to picture the colonial system as it really was. Yet Nkrumah was born into its very heart.

In 1909, when Kwame's father poured libations to his ancestors and said prayers in thanks for the child's safe arrival in this world, the system was still pushing itself powerfully out across the continent. If its frontiers were already marked on maps, the colonial powers had still to make these colonies safe for their system, and it took them a long time to do this. In many colonies there were African wars of resistance as late as Nkrumah's time at Achimota, and sometimes even later still. The last great anti-colonial resistance in the Gold Coast, leading to the final overthrow of the Ashanti Empire, had ended only a few years before his birth.

The whole system was fastened upon Africa during his early lifetime. Its impact varied from place to place, being harshest for Africans wherever there were white settlers who saw themselves as a 'local master race'. There were no such settlers in the Gold Coast. But there were plenty of whites there who saw themselves in the same way: businessmen, police officers, officials, and others of their kind. These might give lip-service to the principle that Africans should have self-rule 'in the end';

few of them believed that this would ever happen. Those were the days when white men in Africa were contemptuous of 'natives', above all when these were educated men. They insisted on their own superiority, and thought that Africans had no history, culture, or civilization of their own.

The resultant atmosphere of cultural suffocation has been well described by a British historian of Africa, Christopher Fyfe, in his biography of the West African scientist and patriot, J. Africanus Horton (1853–83):

In these European possessions whites ruled and non-whites obeyed. All the European empires in Africa were empires of race, where there was little place for an educated African . . . Those [Africans] with professional qualifications were squeezed out of government service and humiliated socially. [Horton's] wife's relative Dr J. F. Easmon was ruthlessly hounded out of his post as Chief Medical Officer, Gold Coast, by a vindictive governor and replaced by a European. Regulations were made in 1902 to constitute a unified West African Medical Service. Africans were specifically excluded from it [only seven years before Nkrumah's birth] and relegated to a separate service, with lower salary scales, so that even the most senior African doctor could not give an order to the most junior white doctor.

Things were better, twenty-five years later, when Nkrumah entered Achimota. It was then a long time since a leading British official had declared that 'the educated native' was 'the curse of the West Coast'. But there were still quite a few local whites who agreed with that opinion. Only two years before Nkrumah's arrival at Achimota, the Gold Coast nationalist J. E. Casely Hayford complained of discrimination in the medical service. 'Until we knocked and knocked and knocked again,' he said, 'the West African Medical Service was a closed door; they did not want us to get in. It was a question whether we were ever going to get in at all.'

Nkrumah had no wish to be a doctor, but the words meant something to every African who cherished a belief in his right to equal treatment with other men; and one of the keys to

Nkrumah's later thought and action can be found here. To the nationalists of those days it became the supreme need to assert and secure this right. They had to demonstrate that Africans could bear the same responsibilities as Europeans. They had to throw off the colonial heritage of 'inferiority'. Before they could hope to be able to do anything else, they had to 'get out from under' the mountain of colonial power.

This became the driving idea of the Ghana of Nkrumah's youth. The great and primary task was to achieve equality of respect and treatment, no matter what might happen next. Only this could restore to Africans the power to control their own history and development. Outstanding men in West Africa had long stated this absolute need. Horton and Blyden and others had done it before 1900. Mensah Sarbah, Casely Hayford and others in Ghana or elsewhere continued the work. Some were brilliant men who would have made their mark anywhere. They became the spokesmen and pioneers of West African nationhood; and Nkrumah was among the younger generation of half a century ago who ardently followed their lead.

*

What kind of lead was it?

These men were also the product of their times, and their times supposed, as ours do not, that worthwhile civilization had to come from Europe. So they were driven to compete with Europeans on European terms. They had to excel in all the subjects which Europeans thought necessary, not least in Greek and Latin. In the measure they succeeded, they had to accept a special status in their own African countries. They had to become a privileged group or élite, even if this divided them from the lives of the majority of their fellow-countrymen. There was no other way for them to develop their skills and exercise their talents.

They were therefore caught in an awkward contradiction. They wished to assert and show the value of Africa's peoples, cultures, civilizations of the past; and that was one thing. But they also looked to Europe for guides and good examples; and that was quite another.

Attoh Ahuma was one of them. His ideas demonstrate this contradiction very well. A distinguished Gold Coast newspaper editor, Attoh Ahuma exhorted his readers to do better than just copy the Europeans, and to love their own country for itself. But this same Attoh Ahuma also wrote: 'Let us help one another to find a way out of Darkest Africa. The impenetrable jungle around us is not darker than the dark primeval forest of the human mind uncultured. We must emerge from the savage back-woods and come into the open where nations are made.' Yet how were his readers to be proud of their country and its heritage, if this was 'a dark primeval forest' of 'savage back-woods'?

The contradiction stayed with the educated group, the élite, in all the years that followed. The men of the élite sincerely wished to 'make the nation', but they thought that only people who were able and willing to take their examples from Europe would be able to do that. Europe had become their 'spiritual home'. So it was to be, in due course, that one of the soldiers who overthrew Nkrumah's rule in 1966, Colonel (then Major) Afrifa, could write of the British military academy of Sandhurst with a boundless admiration not only as a training school but also as a guide to political behaviour. An Englishman might reply that whatever Afrifa may have learned at Sandhurst, he had not learned its sovereign rule about politics: that serving soldiers stay rigorously out of them.

But so it would be, again in due course, that Dr Kofi Busia, leader of the brief regime which followed military rule in 1969, withdrew to live in Oxford when he in turn was overthrown in 1972. There Dr Busia lived in the shadow of England's oldest and perhaps most conservative university, the one that was, in many ways, spiritual father to the British Empire. 'Oxford,' he had once said, long before, 'has made me what I am today.'

Such men desired Ghana's independence, but only if it could be independence 'in the British way', shaped on British models, enjoying British approval, and therefore, by the logic of this attitude, fulfilling Britain's interests. But could British interests be the same as Africa's? It was a question that the educated élite preferred not to consider, much less to answer, whether in colonial times or later.

Nkrumah was trained as a member of this privileged élite; the important point is that he rejected his training. Once through Achimota, climbing the scholarly ladder, he might well have followed the same kind of career as Busia, gaining eventually the grand accolade of an Oxford degree and, with it, the blessing of the imperial establishment. But he chose otherwise.

Eager to travel and know the world, he went to Britain only in later life, and then as a political worker. Meanwhile he chose another country, although this other country was less comfortable for an educated black man, or any kind of black man, even than the bony knees of the 'imperial mother's' lap. And when he came home again at last, twelve years later, this member of the élite had become a man determined to speak for the mass of his fellow countrymen, and to embrace their interests as his own.

It remains that his training as a teacher and university lecturer were always to be a handicap for him. This training gave him the keys to an understanding of his country's condition; but it stood between him and the practicalities of daily life. He was always to know things in theory far better than in practice. All this lay hidden in the future when he took stock of his life in 1935, and wondered what to do next. He had taught school for six years: was he to do it for the rest of his life? The prospect depressed him. Somewhere a life's work lay ahead of him, but this was not it.

Faced with this kind of dilemma, bright young men in the Gold Coast had always gone to Britain when they could: the road to a career had always seemed to lie that way. But these years were the 'stormy Thirties' of West African political development, and many new ideas were on the scene. Agitation for reform had reached a new height only a year earlier, in 1934, when Dr J. B. Danquah had led to London a delegation of protest against three measures which seemed, once again, to confirm the country's eternally colonial position. But for young nationalists in the Gold Coast then, even this lead by Danquah and his friends was put in the shade by the presence of a quite different kind of man, Nnamdi Azikiwe, a Nigerian nationalist lately returned from the United States.

The coming of Azikiwe 'was like an electric shock' to the younger ranks of intellectuals in the Gold Coast, firing their imagination 'for the emancipation from thraldom' by speeches, newspaper articles and private talks.* But 'Zik' pointed the way ahead for these intellectuals in a more personal way as well, urging them 'to go to the United States' and, in words that would become familiar, 'to come back with the Golden Fleece'. Nkrumah was among the first who took the advice. He decided to go to the land which had shaped not only Zik, but also such diverse pioneers as Kwegyir Aggrey, Marcus Garvey and William Du Bois. And there he would find out what should happen to him next.

In Africa there is usually an uncle or a cousin who will help a young man of enterprise and courage. He managed to raise £150 from two relatives; added to some slender savings of his own, it was enough. He went to say goodbye to his mother. The parting was sad, and both were in tears. But his mother had her own ideas about her son and his future. 'It cannot be helped,' she told him, 'may God and your ancestors guide you.'

AMERICA: LEARNING SCHOOL

An African of enterprise and courage thinks nothing nowadays of setting out for Europe or America. Hundreds are doing it every month, flocking into airports crowded with others coming back again. In most foreign countries, the traveller will find his own consulate or embassy, plenty of friends from home and

* As recalled by Professor K. A. P. Jones-Quartey in lectures at Edinburgh University, 1972.

foreign friends, even a tribe of landladies for whom black folk are no longer strange or frightening rarities. Being a 'been to' has long since ceased to be anything to boast about, while university diplomas awarded at home may be an even better ticket to a job than diplomas awarded abroad.

In 1935, and for a long while afterwards, it was not a bit like that. Those who went abroad on scholarships were few; fewer still were those who went, as Nkrumah did, without a scholarship. There were no such things as independent passports, but only colonial passports fit for second-class citizens; and second-class citizens could count on little help from anyone, especially if they were black. They might find charity here and there; respect and friendship could be as rare as freshwater fish in the sea.

Even when the traveller had enterprise and courage, as Nkrumah did, the adventure was still a test of nerves. Every black man or woman who travelled then—but there were few women among the travellers—had to meet and carry the portentous weight of the 'white man's burden', the white man's belief in African inferiority. It was a lonely journey to set out upon, and lonely to continue.

In later life Nkrumah often remembered how he had boarded the *Apapa* at Takoradi, in the Gold Coast which would not become Ghana for another twenty-two years, and 'felt desperately alone and sat on my bunk close to tears'. Yet those who embark upon enterprises of great moment may well find help where they least expect it. Beside him on his bunk he found a telegram. Its words were few: 'Goodbye. Remember to trust in God and in yourself.' But the signature said more. It was that of Nnamdi Azikiwe, the man to whom, above all, he had looked for leadership.

Reading this telegram on his bunk in the *Apapa*, the traveller cheered up and began to count his blessings and 'remind myself', as he wrote much later, 'that this, after all, was the beginning of all that I had planned and saved for'.

Something of the same sort happened in London, where he

went to obtain a visa for the United States, one of the few things easier to get in those days than it is now. London dazed him with its roar and scramble of people and things. London seemed to shout its contempt for anything but itself. Whatever good thing, except a visa, could London offer a lonely traveller from the tropics?

'But just as I was feeling particularly depressed about the future,' he afterwards recalled, 'I heard an excited newspaper boy shouting something unintelligible as he grabbed a bundle of the latest editions from a newspaper van, and on the placard I read: "Mussolini Invades Ethiopia". That was all I needed. At that moment it was almost as if the whole of London had suddenly declared war on me personally. For the next few minutes I could do nothing but glare at each impassive face, wondering if those people could possibly realize the wickedness of colonialism, and praying that the day might come when I could play my part in bringing about the downfall of such a system.' Perhaps he was over-stating what he really felt, as people often do when they remember the big moments in their lives, the turning-points that matter. Yet he must have felt something like that. All his later life bears witness to it.

He went to Liverpool, armed with his American visa, and stayed there for a fortnight with a timber merchant who was the agent of a well-to-do trader of Axim in his own country. There he was introduced to English family life, and found it interesting: wives, for example, could 'answer back' to their husbands without giving offence, much less ground for divorce. It is not at all clear if the youthful Kwame thought this a good thing. Women, for him, remained a dangerous sort of people.

A liner of the old Cunard White Star fleet took him to America in a comfortable cabin. It says much about him, in this period, that aboard ship he made a close friendship with a Dutch student of divinity. After getting to America this Hollander and he stayed in touch, and went to church together. The Nkrumah of this period had still a great deal of the training and belief of his missionary upbringing. Theology and philosophy were high on the list of his interests. Later on, in Philadelphia, he was to mount the pulpit of a Baptist church and preach on Sundays.

He was never to be a great public speaker, but in the more intimate atmosphere of a debate he came really into his own. Here his rather weak voice was no disadvantage; while his bookishness and incessant reading helped to make him impressive. To marshal and carry an argument he still needed much preparation, and this indeed he would always need: his gift was not for off-the-cuff brilliance in discussion. 'He had charm, a sort of delightful gaucherie, explosive mirth, and so on,' Professor Jones-Quartey has recalled of those student days in America. 'But he was plain inarticulate in serious unrehearsed discussion.'* Yet his personality seems already to have marked him out as a man who would lead.

First of all, he had to find a place. He had written from the Gold Coast and then from Liverpool to the Dean of Lincoln University, Pennsylvania, but this was no guarantee of a good reception. Meanwhile he was without money, and two months late for the start of the university year. They admitted him at Lincoln on condition that he could stay only if he did well in the coming examinations for freshmen. He did do well, and received a scholarship.

This was more than a foot in the door of the New World, but the money problem remained. Lincoln's scholarship holders could earn as waiters in the dining-hall or assistants in the library. He was glad to be able to choose the second. Library work and other little jobs, such as 'ghosting' papers for less able or energetic fellow students, kept him going in term-time. The long university holidays were another matter. All through his American years, Nkrumah had to pay his way through the holidays by such menial jobs as he could find.

Some of these jobs were easy enough, others were not. One of them was carting offal in a soap factory; he stood it for two weeks. For three successive summers he went to sea as a waiter

* Edinburgh lectures, 1972.

on ships. But the winters were worst. In the bitter cold of one of these, soon after passing his degree of Master of Arts at the University of Philadelphia, he got a job in a shipbuilding yard. There, he recalled in his autobiography written fourteen years later, 'I worked in all weathers from twelve midnight until eight the following morning. It froze so hard on several occasions that my hands almost stuck to the steel and although I put on all the clothes I possessed, I was chilled to the marrow.' The sheltered intellectual was not only learning school, but life as well; and he was learning it the hard way.

Yet this serious young man in metal-rimmed glasses was very much an intellectual, no matter what sweat-stained toil he might endure in the holidays. Higher education suited him. He liked its theoretical and speculative sides. He soared through examinations. In 1939 he graduated from Lincoln with a degree in economics and sociology, and was briefly attracted by the idea of a career in journalism. Generations of outstanding West Africans had edited or written for newspapers, and journalism was one of his interests. But he lacked the money to pay the necessary fees to Columbia University's school of journalism.

Lincoln offered him an assistant lectureship in theology and philosophy. Desperately short of cash, he accepted. It was not, he said, 'what I had planned for myself', but it was a useful port in the financial storm that raged about him. Assistant lecturers were also expected to improve their time by more learning, and this suited him too. He had a passion for learning. He would always have a passion for learning.

He began to read philosophy. It was 'respectable' philosophy, since no other was welcomed through the portals of a Western university in those days. Thus he mentions having read the works of Kant, Descartes, Schopenhauer, Nietsche, Freud and others; but it is doubtful if the 'others' included Marx or Plekhanov, Lenin or any other revolutionary. Later on he read some of these as well, but Lincoln's training in idealist philosophy wove another strand into his mental fabric, and this remained with him in after years.

B

He was no kind of revolutionary at this stage. Far from that, he was an enthusiastic theologian. He began working for a degree in theology, and received this in 1942 at the head of his class. Meanwhile he had moved to the University of Philadelphia where, again in 1942 and providing another proof of his stubborn energy, he achieved a master's degree in education. When in later life he was awarded an honorary doctorate, a title which he at once affixed before his name, he could reasonably claim that he had earned it.

He was now more highly educated than most citizens of Europe and America in those days, not to speak of Africans. The gateway to a lifetime's pleasant well-paid employment as a university lecturer, and eventually professor, was fully open to him. He could have stayed quietly in the United States, and retired upon a safe and comfortable pension.

Why didn't he do it? One can point to several answers. All are important, but the most important is that the light of a very different ambition was already leading him. Its illumination came from various directions. But ever more clearly, as he now began to understand, these pointed the same way.

AMERICA: LEARNING LIFE

Perhaps he would have stayed quietly in the United States, climbing the rungs of an academic career, if the stability and comforts of that kind of life had much appealed to him. In obvious ways, of course, they did appeal. He enjoyed a good meal and security of income as well as the next man. He had little of either, not only because he was a black man in America but also because America had still to recover from the miseries of economic slump, at least until 1942.

Yet a professorial life meant settling down; and settling down, among other things, meant marriage. Any thought of marriage conjured up his anxiety about women. He formed several friendships with women in the United States and some of them appear to have been intimate; but he made sure they never lasted. In his attitudes to women he swayed between fear and arrogance. It was an unhappy side of his character, and he never overcame its emotional immaturity.

Or again, perhaps he would have stayed if his sojourn in the United States had occurred at a somewhat earlier stage of history. Then he might have settled there, as many other talented Africans had done, conserving the hope of change in the black man's lot while not quite believing in it. He might have joined America's 'black bourgeoisie', content with the crumbs of dignity and status that white America let fall. He might have retained an interest in Africa as a distant subject, and spoken, again without quite believing in it as a practical possibility, of Africa's right to equality and justice.

But his years in America happened to be years of great change up and down the world. He had marked its signs even before leaving home. He had listened to Nnamdi Azikiwe, read West African newspapers which dared the colonial laws of sedition with the sting and savour of their protest, lived in the heady atmosphere of early nationalism. He had not in the least forgotten any of that.

There was all that; and there was more. The last years of his stay in the United States were also those of the world war against the alliance of Hitler's regime in Germany and Mussolini's in Italy. The Western allies and the Soviet Union fought for their national survival; but little by little the war became more than a defence of those countries, or of others occupied by the Nazi-Fascist armies. Gradually it also became a war against the 'old order', even against any kind of imperialism, as well as against the racism of Hitler and Mussolini. Colonial Asia was resurgent; soon Africa might be the same. It seemed not to be a time for settling into a quiet and respectable career.

Such thoughts were reinforced by others. He was not looking far ahead at this stage; there was nothing to encourage him in doing so. But he was looking closely at the world around him. And everything it told him appeared to be in conflict with the notion of a retreat behind university walls.

One source of enlightenment came from writers and leaders of opinion who stood in the long line of those who had struggled for black emancipation in America. He had known some of these by name before leaving home, and had read some of their writings. At their head stood Marcus Garvey and William Du Bois, powerful though strongly different pioneers whose fame had long since reached the colonies of Africa. Now he discovered the works of many others, and read them avidly.

He found two schools of thought among the blacks in America. By far the more influential held that black Americans had long since lost any connection they might once have had with Africa. Their future, on this view, could lie only in becoming so completely American, in all their ideas or ambitions, that white Americans would accept them as equal citizens. Africa, for this school of thought, was the 'savage backwoods' of which Attoh Ahuma had written a quarter of a century earlier. Black Americans—or Negroes, as they then called themselves, adopting another white habit—could only worsen their chances of a decent life if they harped on any 'African connection'. Better forget the Dark Continent, and its shameful stain! *

The second school of thought held an opposite view. William Du Bois, Leo Hansberry and others had long argued that black people in America could realize their full humanity only if they accepted their African heritage. They should be proud of Africa and its history. And they would be proud of it, if only they knew what this history was. These men set out to study and to teach the history of Africa. If in a small way as yet, 'Negro studies' also began to become 'African studies'.

Nkrumah joined this second school of thought, as did other students from Africa; and the study of African history became another of his life's interests. Deeply influenced by the ideas of Du Bois, he began to develop his belief in Pan-Africanism, in black unity, and this was to be another of the formative influences of his American years. If the ex-colonies of North

* 'American Negroes wanted nothing to do with Africa in those days': Professor Jones-Quartey, Edinburgh lectures, 1972.

America had needed to become a federation of united states before growing great and powerful, then Africa, he began to argue, would surely have to do the same.

He argued for this conviction, and soon was deep in conflict with other students. Among these the Gold Coasters generally took his side, but the Nigerians, led by a tremendously energetic 'Ibo group' among whom Kingsley Mbadiwe was already prominent, thought that Nkrumah's ideas about African unity were at this stage absurdly unrealistic, and said so in many scorching arguments. Such arguments were to continue far into the future, and fill Nkrumah's later life with hot and often harsh disputes.

He taught Negro history at the University of Philadelphia. But Negro history was primarily American history, and this satisfied him no more than it satisfied other African students. What about their own history? What about their present and their future? Nkrumah helped to set up an African studies section. He went further, and helped to organize an African students' association as a place for meeting and debate. This rapidly became political debate. It formed Nkrumah's entry into practical politics. The association elected him as its president, and published an occasional newspaper, the *African Interpreter*. 'We tried,' he wrote afterwards, 'to revive a spirit of nationalism.'

All this gave light about how things were and how they might be made to become: illumination about colonial Africa and the possibilities of freedom. It was not a clear light nor a strong one; but it was there, and it counted. Meanwhile the realities of everyday life brought a stronger source of light. It, too, came from various directions.

One of these derived from the pain of being black, and above all a poor black, in the America of the 1930s and 1940s. Coming from home, this had surprised him. White men ruled the Gold Coast, and sometimes with a contempt for Africans, but white men there were few and far between, and 'everyday racism' was a thing unknown. He found it a daily wretchedness here.

He used to say that his first experience of aggressive racism happened in Baltimore. 'I was parched with thirst and I entered the refreshment room,' during a bus trip, and 'asked the white American waiter if I could have a drink of water. He frowned and looked down his nose at me as if I was something unclean. "The place for you, my man, is the spittoon outside," he declared as he dismissed me from his sight. I was so shocked that I could not move.'

Nkrumah learned to take that kind of thing with the rest. Being educated, and therefore to all appearances a 'respectable Negro', he suffered from such insults less than most blacks. But he also learned how others suffered more; and what he learned about 'white supremacy' in those years stayed with him. It helped to form and conserve the deep convictions that he came to hold on the evils of colonialism as a form of race rule.

In Philadelphia, at one point, he was employed by the Presbyterian Church to carry out a survey of how local black people lived, and what they believed, and how much money they had. He went into hundreds of black homes, and learned the black American story from the inside. He was learning to understand the white American story as well, but not as told in the tourist literature or in patriotic history books. He saw the massive unemployment of whites as well as blacks, the dreadful housing conditions in which many whites had to live, the country's poverty as well as its pride. Back at home the schools had taught about the white man's world as though it were a paradise where everyone was rich and happy. The truth, he found, was different.

This led him into new channels of thought. He began to read philosophers other than the ones recommended at Lincoln: revolutionary writers who challenged the social and imperialist system of which America, like Britain, was a major part. He began to consider Marx and Engels and Lenin. Not very thoroughly, it appears, but enough to let him see that an alternative to that system was at least thinkable. It seems unlikely that he got beyond a nodding acquaintance with Marxist ideas, or at this stage could discuss them in more than slogans. That was evidently the opinion of the most important of the black revolutionary thinkers whom he met in the United States, the Trinidadian C. L. R. James. Nkrumah 'used to talk about imperialism and Leninism and export of capital,' James recalled a quarter of a century later, 'and he used to talk a lot of nonsense.'* But then so do most people who become aware of revolutionary ideas for the first time. Such ideas tend to go to honest people's heads. Some of them went to Nkrumah's; some of them settled there, but there he grappled with them and made them his own.

When the second world war drew to a close, it was clearly time to go. He had long thought about leaving, but travel during the war was difficult and it was better to wait. By 1945 he was waiting with impatience. Finally, in May of that year, he sailed from New York after ten American years packed with hard work and, as he said afterwards, also with a lot of happiness.

So there he is, aged thirty-six, a very different man from the young student who landed in New York in 1935. New York harbour fades in the western wind as the pinnacles of Manhattan Island dwindle out of sight. Another world lies in front, a world that is also greatly different from the one he left ten years before. 'I was no longer,' he would write in his autobiography, 'the ardent youth setting out on a strange venture, inexperienced and easily shocked by the ways of the western world. Ten years in America had seen to that.'

He is now a mature man, and strongly formed in his beliefs and ambitions. He wants to help in freeing his country. He believes that he can play a part in that, perhaps a big part: as James will tell Padmore in a letter of introduction, 'he's determined to throw the Europeans out of Africa.' But how does he think he is going to do that, as he bids farewell to the Statue of Liberty on the ocean passage from New York? What dreams and visions drive him now?

* Quoted from *Radical America*, vol. 2, no. 4, 1963, pp. 24–7, by T. Martin, 'C. L. R. James and the Race/Class Question' in *Race*, London, vol. 14, no. 2, October 1972, p. 183.

These questions had better be considered here, for once he gets to the eastern side of the ocean there will be little time to pause and think. The tides of fortune will sweep him onward from one scene of action to the next. What he is thinking now, about the deeper purposes of his life, will largely remain what he will think later. These ideas and convictions he carries with him will help to explain his dazzling success. They will also help to explain his downfall.

HOMEWARD BOUND

A deck chair in the shelter of a liner's funnel is a good place to sit and think, or sit and dream, as long as there's a blanket to wrap around your knees against the chill May winds of the north Atlantic. There is no racism aboard this liner, or none that is organized; and anyone who pays his passage may sit in a deck chair. Besides, why disturb a respectable Negro who just sits and thinks, with a book on his lap and several more beside him on the deck?

Nobody bothers him. He neither drinks nor smokes, retaining habits of personal abstention that date back to his training and his poverty, but also to his preference for simple living. He chats pleasantly when spoken to, and his gentle manners are admired by some and wondered at by others. The way he talks English is still marked by the accents of West African schooling, where he learned the language from African teachers who had learned it from other African teachers. He has little or nothing of an American twang.

He talks when in the mood, but mostly he keeps to himself. There is little he can share with these passengers returning to a war-ravaged England and concerned with what they will find there. He is concerned with quite other matters, and these give him plenty of food for thought.

Two great ideas dominate his mind. The first is an old one, long cherished; many share it with him. It is the idea that what Africans must now do, first and foremost and before anything else can be seriously discussed, is to 'get out from under' the colonial mountain. They have to push off colonial rule before they can stand up straight, start a new life of their own, work for their own good, recover their place in world history. Before the second world war this mountain appeared so tall and heavy that nobody would ever be able to push it off. But now, in 1945, it seems to have lost a lot of its height and weight. There may be a chance for Africans, even a good chance.

But he thinks of his second idea perhaps even more. This second idea is above all the fruit of his stay in the United States. It moves him with the vigour of a vision, and carried him far from the liner's deck, opening up the splendid future of a United Africa, an Africa of united states, a federation of hundreds of millions of black people who stride upon the world's scene with all the force of their numbers and talents, skills and strength.

It is an American vision, above all the creation of black people in the Americas. Cut off from their distant homeland, deprived of their own separate African cultures, languages and loyalties, black thinkers in the Americas came easily to the conclusion that differences between black people were far less important than the fact that all of them were black, and, being black, united in their interests. But if this was true about black people in the Americas, these thinkers concluded, then it must also be true of black people in Africa. If the first could save themselves only by uniting their strength, then the resurgence of Africa must take the road of a similar unity.

There are few people today who will doubt the essential truth of this. But there are many who understand, far better than twenty years ago, that the building of unity must be a long and difficult task. Yet in 1945 the obstacles were far from obvious to black Americans who believed in Africa's resurgence. They discounted the colonial obstacles to unity, and also the purely African obstacles. They tended to believe that all Africans regarded each other as brothers. Push away the colonial mountain, and all Africans would then be as one nation.

Thus the pioneer of the Pan-African idea, William Du Bois,

had declared way back in 1900 that the main problem of the twentieth century was the problem of the colour line. Later in his life he came to see that he had been wrong in thinking this. The colour problem was important, and would remain important; but it was not, as he later argued, the main problem. The main problem was the problem that made the colour line important; and this was the problem of economic and political system, the problem of historical development. In some words of C. L. R. James, expressing the same conviction, 'the race question is subsidiary to the class question in politics, and to think of imperialism in terms of race is disastrous', although 'neglect of the racial factor as merely incidental', James added, 'is an error only less grave than to make it fundamental'.* But this was revolutionary thinking, and Nkrumah was not, or not yet, a revolutionary.

Yet he was also not a black American. In character and talent, he was very much a man of Ghana. He knew from his own homeland, as well as from his studies, that Africans were divided amongst themselves by much more than the divisions of colonial rule. They were divided by their languages, old loyalties, different interests, various rivalries. They were divided into chiefs and commoners, townsmen and countrymen, a few rich and many poor, and by much else besides. Later on, through much bitter experience, he would come to know this better still.

But it seems clear that his years in the United States, his faith in Pan-Africanism, his own internationalist sense of belonging to the world and not simply to some small part of the world, all tended to obscure for him the depth and diversity of Africa's divisions. It seemed right and reasonable to him that Africa, once freed from foreign rule, should rapidly unite under a single federal government. It was a view that vastly oversimplified reality, but he never abandoned it. His first great idea, the freeing of Ghana from colonial rule, remained always the servant of the second. Ghana's independence, he was to say,

* C. L. R. James, *The Black Jacobins*, reprinted New York, 1963, p. 283.

would be meaningless if it were not to be linked with the total liberation of Africa.

This is the field of thought that yields another key to his mind and mood. Coming back across the Atlantic, returning to England so as to prepare for returning home, he is already a man of ideas far more than a man of practical politics. He will transform himself into a man of action, and will prove to be repeatedly successful as one, but he will stay essentially what he is now: a man moved above all else by a world-changing vision. In an Africa desperately needing such a vision, much of his renown will flow from this.

The visionary nature of his thought comes out in much else that he says and does in these months. Returning from America, he is an intellectual who has still to 're-Africanize' himself, who has still to test his ideas against the gritty problems of everyday life. He partly knows this, and partly ignores it. He is a man standing on the brink of an ocean of storms, peering far away to the other side and charting an ideal course to cross it by the shortest route. The vision of what can lie beyond repeatedly urges him forward. Far more than any personal ambition, this 'lack of realism' was the price that he and his people had to pay for the privilege of leading black Africa on the road to political independence. Considering some of the 'realists' who sit in high places today, perhaps it was no high price to pay.

As yet, returning home across the Atlantic, his further ideas on what to do, and how to do it, are still in a confusion. In 1957 he would describe himself as 'a non-denominational Christian and a Marxist socialist'. Now he might say much the same, yet it would be little more than a declaration of loyalty to the ideas of far-reaching change. In America he read some of the Marxist classics and dabbled in many philosophies. It seems they have given him no clear guide to action. He remains above all a pragmatist, a man who will act according to opportunities, leaving great principles to save themselves by the sheer force of their own logic. It will be his strength as well as his weakness.

Otherwise he has learned in the school of everyday American life that nothing worthwhile can be had except by work, and organization: above all, by organization. But he tends to see organization as one thing, and the ideas that should guide action as quite another. He does not really bring the two together. His notion is rather that you have objectives, select the best for your immediate purpose, and then organize people to carry them out. He is a revolutionary 'from the top down'. Much in his writings shows this.

Thus he says of meeting C. L. R. James that in this way 'he learned how an underground movement worked'. But James could only tell him in theory; he could not demonstrate in practice, for there was no underground movement, or none that was effective. It was rather as if, in order to launch an 'underground movement', you needed only to know a set of rules. His first political pamphlet, published later under the title of 'Towards Colonial Freedom', is little more than a collection of such theoretical 'rules'.

The national liberation movement in the African colonies, [he wrote in 1945] has arisen because of the continuous economic and political exploitation by foreign oppressors. The aim of the movement is to win freedom and independence. This can only be achieved by the political education and organization of the colonial masses. Hence workers and professional classes alike must unite on a common front to further the economic progress and indigenous enterprise of the people which is at present being stifled.

It might still be useful to publish such slogan-like utterances in the colonial world of 1945. But they were far removed from the patient and particular analysis of practical reality, on the spot, which can alone support a revolutionary effort. At this stage, in other words, Nkrumah has some revolutionary ideas, but that is all.

In 1945, however, it could seem a very revolutionary thing merely to say that Africa should be independent. Anyone who said it loud and clear was likely to be treated by the authorities as a public danger. Such persons were noted down as subversives, chivvied out of jobs when they had any, or denied jobs when they had none. Colonial power acted on the principle that any connection with Marxism, any acquaintance with revolutionary ideas, was sufficient proof of natural wickedness and base disloyalty. Nkrumah would be duly entered in the files as a dangerous man. He would take it all with wry humour, his eyes upon the future.

He arrives in England with one clear objective. He wants to get into the action. But where is the action, and who is conducting it? He knows only one man in England who may be likely to put him on the right road. He writes to this unknown friend, a West Indian of strong nationalist views, to ask him if he will meet the traveller at the London railway station on arrival. It is a long shot, but it works. The ancestors, as his mother might have said, have not forgotten him.

He gets out of the train and George Padmore is there to meet him. A friendship develops that will count for much in later years. Padmore takes him to the hostel of the West African Students' Union. After a few days there Nkrumah finds its atmosphere confining, and sets out to find a bed-sitting room where he can be more private. London landladies, he discovers, do not like 'coloured men'; the search proves long. But one day it ends happily at a little house in Tufnell Park, one of those lost suburbs of North London where 'nobody lives' save the people who live there. At 60 Burleigh Road the search for a temporary home is at last successful. The family is a kindly one; they like him and they look after him, and he will not forget their kindness.

'I was rarely in before midnight as I used to work until all hours. But whatever time I came in I always knew that I would find something to eat left for me in the oven. In return for all their kindness I insisted that my landlady leave all the dirty dishes for me to wash. I did this regularly before I went to bed.' He was good at washing dishes; he had done it often for a meagre wage in the United States and aboard American ships at sea. Now he did it for nothing. It was a 'lack of realism' of a kind which might with advantage be wider spread about the world.

Thus established, he was ready to begin.

LONDON INTERLUDE

The records offer glimpses of the man in the two years of his stay in England, 1945–47, but no detailed memoirs. Many encountered him, for he mixed in political life, but few came to know him well. The glimpses of that period show him much as he long remained: a slender, restless figure with a multitude of interests and a great impatience to pursue them all.

Perhaps the best physical description, though referring to a few years later, is that of Richard Wright, the black American writer. Nkrumah, in Wright's words, 'was fairly slightly built, a smooth jet black in colour; he had a largish face, a pair of brooding, almost frightened eyes, a set of full soft lips. His head held a thick growth of crinkly hair and his hands moved with slow restlessness, betraying a contained tension.' It is the portrayal of a man whose mind warred continually with his heart, and who knew, and accepted, that the mission he had set himself could not be an easy or a safe one. Courage is what a man does in spite of fear. Nkrumah had plenty of courage.

His impact on the small black community then in London, or on that still smaller part of it involved in political debate, was soon felt. It is easy to see why, even setting the man's qualities aside. The end of the war was opening new horizons. New men were needed, new ideas. Even in 1945 it was clear that the British empire was about to be ended on the Indian sub-continent; if there, why not in Africa? In the middle of the year, soon after Nkrumah's arrival, the British electorate returned the Labour Party to power with a large majority. There were influential people in the Labour Party who were ready to press for reform in Africa as well as in Britain.

Leading Africans and West Indians then in London marked the moment well. They welcomed Nkrumah as a promising recruit. He was absolutely an African, but he also had an intellectual self-confidence that came from his long years in the United States. He had escaped from the provincial narrowness of the 'colonial condition'. He was obviously ambitious, but for more than himself, perhaps for much more. He was an educated man, but he soon made it clear that he was also ready to labour at the humble work of political organization, and, if necessary, to go hungry in doing so.

He enjoyed his London days, and again it is easy to see why. There was powerfully about him the atmosphere of a world to win. It seemed like the dawn of a new age, and all the brighter because it was set in the drab grey poverty of a city ravaged by bombing and the strains of war, of a country which had put forth its last strength to survive and win, and was now turning its back on the past, confusedly searching for a life that would be different.

Happily based in Burleigh Road, Nkrumah threw himself into many activities. He put down his name at Gray's Inn, one of the great law centres. He put down his name for lectures in economics at the University of London. A little later he put down his name for lectures in philosophy as well, and was admitted as a candidate for London's doctorate in philosophy.

He attended a few of these lectures, but had no time to persevere. Too many other interests plucked at him. Professor Sir Alfred Ayer, the distinguished philosopher who admitted him as a candidate, has told me that Nkrumah was popular in the philosophy department, where he was known as a Hegelian. 'But I can't honestly say,' Sir Alfred comments, 'that I thought Nkrumah a first-class philosopher. I liked him and enjoyed talking to him but he did not seem to me to have an analytical mind. He wanted the answers too quickly. I think part of the trouble may have been that he wasn't concentrating very hard on his thesis. It was a way of marking time until the opportunity came for him to return to Ghana.' Later, when news of his achievements in Ghana began to filter back to London, Ayer was one of many who had met him who were understandably surprised that this political leader was the man whom they had known.

Others in his own community were also surprised, but less so. At the West African Students' Union, then a lively place, he was soon at the centre of discussion about Africa's future. Into this debate he plunged with all his fervour, but found time for practical things as well. Elected as the Union's vice-president, he helped members through troubles arising from shortages of cash, aggressive landladies, and the like.

He met a lot of politicians, mainly Liberal and Labour but also some Communists. Several impressed him by their awareness of the need for African liberation, even if they had few practical ideas on how this might be brought about. He further developed his ideas about socialism, talking with colleagues such as Bankole Awooner-Renner, though still in a very theoretical way. But almost from the first he was drawn by another attraction. A meeting of the Pan-African Congress, the sixth since Du Bois and others had held the first in 1900, was planned for October 1945, so as to review the situation of colonial Africa in the light of the war's ending and its possible consequences. With two West Indian friends, George Padmore and T. R. Makonnen, and a South African Coloured writer, Peter Abrahams, Nkrumah became involved in the work of organizing for this congress. Acting as joint secretary with Padmore, his task was to ensure that as many black organizations as possible were informed about the event. This meant discovering what organizations existed and who could be found to represent them at the Congress. None of this was easy when so little was known in London about what was happening in Africa.

The congress met in Manchester, and proved a memorable one. It was presided over by the venerable Du Bois himself, seventy-three years old but still very active and sharp of tongue. Some who were present became famous in later years apart from Nkrumah; among these was Jomo Kenyatta, who was to be the first president of an independent Kenya nearly twenty years later.

Its meetings were marked by a tone fitted to the times. Speaking for Africa's colonized peoples, the congress declared that:

We are not ashamed to have been an age-long patient people. We continue willingly to sacrifice and strive. But we are unwilling to starve any longer while doing the world's drudgery, in order to support by our poverty and ignorance a false aristocracy and a discarded imperialism. We are determined to be free.

That was one note; there was another, the Pan-African note. 'We demand for Black Africa autonomy and independence, so far, and no further, than it is possible in this One World for groups and peoples to rule themselves subject to inevitable world unity and federation.' It spoke for Nkrumah's own conviction.

How far it spoke for the conviction of others, aside from Du Bois himself, is another matter. To a large extent this was the first Pan-African Congress to concern itself with the idea of African unity, as distinct from the idea of black unity across the world. Yet the struggle for independence, as it turned out, was to go in quite a different direction: into a struggle for independence within the separate frontiers drawn on Africa's map by the colonial powers. Most of the members who later achieved power were to forget their Pan-Africanism. Becoming president of Kenya, Kenyatta was to go to war with neighbouring Somalia over the national ownership of semi-desert country near Kenya's northern border. Even Nkrumah, for whom the idea of a federal Africa remained firm and clear, would have to devote much energy to national boundary disputes with Ghana's neighbours.

Generally, his thoughts about the future were reinforced by his stay in England. He stuck to his Pan-Africanism; he sided strongly with the 'revolutionaries' against the 'reformists' in London's African student community. Much of his effort went into writing: already in September 1945, for example, he was writing home to Ghana about the need for 'resolute and audacious' journalism which could 'serve the aspirations' of

West Africa's peoples.* He began to formulate a broad programme or set of working principles: as it finally crystallized,
this was the product of a little sect under Nkrumah's leadership
which called itself the Circle, its membership being limited to
activists of the newly-formed West African National Secretariat,
an obscure and short-lived 'pressure group' which developed
from the Manchester Congress.

The Circle pledged itself in secrecy to work and stay together
'as the Revolutionary Vanguard of the struggle for West African
Unity and National Independence', as well as 'to support the
idea and claims of the All West African National Congress in
its struggle to create and maintain a Union of African Socialist
Republics'. All this was nothing if not visionary. The All West
African National Congress had no existence save on paper, and
scarcely even there, while the aim of creating socialist republics
in Africa, let alone uniting them, must have seemed exceedingly
remote even to the members of the Circle. But it was always
Nkrumah's belief that if you set up an aim you had better set
it high. In this verbalist extremism he was possibly influenced
by Bankole Awooner-Renner, who had worked for a while in
the Soviet-dominated Comintern, and who, in 1946, published
in London a pamphlet entitled 'The West African Soviet
Republic', a vague statement of revolutionary aims whose
thirty-one pages included the Declaration of Independence of
the United States.†

The Circle's secret manifesto afterwards added to Nkrumah's
troubles. Having duly arrested him, the Gold Coast police got
hold of it, and a subsequent commission of inquiry insisted that
it was circumstantial evidence of Nkrumah's possessing communist convictions. As they reproduced the words, the Circle
advocated a union of African *Soviet* Socialist Republics: of
republics, that is, modelled on Russia's example and so, they
argued, under Russia's control.

* See S. K. B. Asante, 'The Aborigines Society, Kwame Nkrumah, and
the 1945 Pan-African Congress', in *Research Review* of the Institute of
African Studies, University of Ghana, vol. 7, no. 2.

† W.A.N.S. Press, London, 1946.

Nkrumah was in truth nothing of a communist, and his understanding of the meaning of socialism was to advance beyond mere theory only in much later years; even then, his thinking was to grapple very seldom with the practical problems of socialist transformation in an African setting. But at least he was freeing himself from the notion that African development must simply be a copy of the development of Western Europe or America. Many other Africans in Europe were also doing this. Most of them abandoned such 'dangerous thoughts' after getting home again, and Nkrumah had to do the same. But although he threw his socialism overboard, he kept a firm line attached to it and later hauled it up again. There will be much to say about that.

And just as he had refused to remain a 'respectable Negro' in the United States, so now he refused to see his future as a member of the 'respectable élite' in Africa. A respectable career would have been easy for him. His academic qualifications were outstanding in the Gold Coast, or in any part of colonial Africa. He could have quickly found a comfortable senior job in teaching or the civil service, and sure promotion would have followed. He could have become 'a good boy', in the jargon of those years, and Authority would have loved him for it. But Nkrumah stayed with his vision.

In spite of all his activities in London, he knew that he was still on the fringe of the action. The real action could only be at home. But how to get into that? It was a tough question, to which the answer came from an unexpected quarter.

'COME BACK AND HELP US'

Boarding a London bus one day in 1945 during his search for lodgings, he had met an old fellow-student of his days at Lincoln University. The two Ghanaians were delighted to see each other. They had worked together on producing the *African Interpreter*, and shared much the same ideas about politics. The difference was that Ako Adjei took them less seriously than

Nkrumah, and was concentrating on bar examinations which were to open his career as a lawyer. Nkrumah let his studies slide; he had too much else to do.

But they were friends as well as fellow-countrymen, and that was pleasant in those lonely months. Ako Adjei helped him to look for lodgings, and together they found Nkrumah's haven in Burleigh Road. Then they lost sight of each other, Adjei returning to Accra to launch his law practice. A year passed, and then most of another year. Nkrumah was impatient by now to get home at last. Yet an absence of twelve years left him hesitant about returning unless he had some clear idea, beforehand, of what he might be able to do when he got there.

A letter came from Ako Adjei. It made a remarkable offer. Would Nkrumah come back to be general secretary of a new nationalist party then about to be launched upon the public scene, the United Gold Coast Convention (U.G.C.C.)? This offer, Adjei explained, was being made with the approval of the leaders of the U.G.C.C. They were men of substance and social position. But just because of this they had few ties with the mass of ordinary folk. What they needed, Adjei had urged upon them, was a man such as Nkrumah who would be able to do something to close the gap between these leaders and the mass support they wished to win.

Nkrumah was doubtful. The newly formed executive of the United Gold Coast Convention, Adjei also explained, would pay Nkrumah a hundred pounds a month, good money in those days, and provide him with a car for organizing work. 'The money and the car didn't interest me so much,' he noted afterwards, although he was practically penniless at the time and could barely feed himself, let alone pay the fare to Accra. 'The job of general secretary, however, most certainly did.' Wasn't this the opportunity he was waiting for?

And yet he hesitated. What was really going forward in the Gold Coast? What could be expected of these 'respectable Negroes' who had formed this new party, the U.G.C.C.? Wouldn't he risk, if he accepted, simply becoming a cog in the well-oiled machine of 'high up' politics between the British colonial authorities and their African 'partners', the country's chiefs and men of substance?

A chance meeting with an Englishman convinced him, he says in his autobiography, that 'it would be quite useless to associate myself with a movement backed almost entirely by reactionaries, middle-class lawyers and merchants'. This Englishman, Tony Maclean, had been working in the Gold Coast for the department of extra-mural studies lately formed by another Englishman, Thomas Hodgkin, who was then the director of extra-mural studies at the University of Oxford, and who, across the coming years, was to become a major figure in the worldwide move towards a reassessment of the value of African history and culture. Nkrumah says that Maclean told him what he thought about the leaders of the U.G.C.C.; and that this confirmed Nkrumah's doubts. He concluded that he would be wasting his time; worse, he would be missing his opportunity to work for rapid and far-going change in the Gold Coast.

Another letter came, this time from Dr J. B. Danquah, moving spirit of the U.G.C.C. and a man of erudition and repute as a lawyer and spokesman for African dignity. Danquah appealed to Nkrumah to set aside his work in London, and come home at once. The need was urgent. What to do? Danquah was undoubtedly a 'middle-class lawyer' of the type that Nkrumah most distrusted. Yet it was possibly an important offer. He asked for advice from his friends and fellow-workers in the West African National Secretariat. 'It might be our beginning,' was the general thought, 'but it could also be our end.' A meeting decided, on balance, that he should go.

So it was that he sailed from Liverpool in November 1947 with many doubts about the people who were to employ him. Had those people then known more about him, they would have returned these doubts. Would they have withdrawn their offer? It is hard to guess. Probably they thought that if Nkrumah proved awkward they could soon bring him to heel. They were influential men who were immensely sure of their own superiority over the mass of their fellow-countrymen. Theirs was to be a rude awakening.

Having accepted their offer, Nkrumah had nothing more to hold him back. With his friend Kojo Botsio he went up to Liverpool and embarked on the *Accra*. For better or for worse, as he appears to have thought while nursing his doubts, the great enterprise was launched.

2. Grappling With Reality

No tribal rabble will sweep us from our positions.
A good old chief in that time.

THE GOOD OLD CHIEFS AND THE DRAGON

He found a country heaving with the tides of change. Staying with relatives in the little western town of Tarkwa, before going up to Accra and beginning his job, he heard the first news of the great shoppers' boycott of European and Middle Eastern traders organized by an Accra chief, Nii Kwabena Bonne.*

This boycott was aimed at bringing down the prices of imported goods, and was not, at least on the surface, a political campaign. The established nationalists of the United Gold Coast Convention, the new party then about to be launched with Nkrumah as its general secretary, had nothing to do with it. If anything, Dr Danquah and his colleagues disapproved of any 'direct action' that could inspire the active participation of ordinary folk. They did not like ordinary folk, and they did not trust them.

But in the atmosphere of 1947 the shoppers' boycott organized by Nii Bonne had a sharp political tune to it; and this chimed with other notes of discontent that were now beginning to be heard. Large numbers of demobilized soldiers had lately returned from the battlefields of Africa and Asia, where they had learned their own lessons about the world. Many of them were eager for political action. In this eagerness they were joined by the spokesmen of young people—of the 'youngmen' as they were called—who were now leaving elementary schools; many of

* His baptismal name was Taylor, and he was originally a Sierra Leonian.

these were discontented with the country's colonial plight. It was not long before Nkrumah began to see the outline of a possible mass movement in support of political change now or in the near future.

That was not how the British authorities saw the situation. They heard the tunes of discontent, of course; their police agents saw to that. And they were ready to make political concessions. But these concessions they were determined to make at their own convenience, and in favour of the 'political class' they recognized, certainly not in favour of the 'mob'. Such concessions would ensure 'continuity': would ensure, that is, the safeguarding of imperial interests.

They thought, too, that there was no particular hurry. For them, the Gold Coast was still the 'model British colony' of imperial tradition, its people happy with their lot and the men of its 'political class' well content to gleam, as in the past, as modest jewels in Britannia's crown, satisfied with an occasional knighthood or a walk up the red carpet at Buckingham Palace.

The British also believed that they were moving with the times, and fast enough to contain the agitations of the immediate postwar period. Only a year earlier, in 1946, they had introduced a new constitution, the first change of this kind for twenty-one years. This new constitution of Governor Burns, it was thought, would fully satisfy the ambitions of the 'political class'. Didn't it, after all, provide for Africans to elect their own representatives to the colonial legislature? And were these not to number as many as eighteen?

This assembly, true enough, would still be a colonial assembly. It could decide or do nothing save with the Governor's consent. As before, the Governor remained the source of power. Yet the 'political class'—the chiefs and lawyers and businessmen who were seen by the British as Britain's successors in ruling the country—would gain at least a voice in what was said in the legislature; and that, it was believed, would probably be quite enough for a long time to come. It was therefore expected that this Burns Constitution of 1946 would last for many years until, perhaps around 1970 or so, another cautious step towards African self-rule might be allowed. Events soon proved the expectation wrong. Within two years of its publication this constitution was practically a dead letter; and within another year it was swept away.

Britain's partners of the 'political class' made the same wrong estimate of how things really were. They saw the tides of mass opinion more clearly than the British, better marked the meaning of the shoppers' boycott, were closer to the impatient voices of the soldiers who had returned from oversea. They knew more fully what the youngmen were saying and thinking: the 'verandah boys', as these were contemptuously called, who 'slept on the verandah' because they had no beds of their own.

But they were great chiefs or the relatives of great chiefs or the henchmen of great chiefs, and they knew the history of their country. The great chiefs had always ruled Ghana, directly in pre-colonial times or indirectly as the servants or collaborators of the British. They were confident about continuing to rule the country in the future: no flotsam and jetsam of the streets and marketplace were going to matter in the long run, or even in the short. Any worthwhile progress, they were sure, could rest only with the advancement of themselves, the 'political class' whom the British recognized and accepted as Britain's successors. Their attitude was common to such people in those times. 'No tribal rabble,' declared a Nigerian member of Nigeria's High Court in a characteristic statement of the period, 'will sweep us from our positions.'

They believed this in 1947, when Nkrumah came home again, and they went on believing it through all the tumultuous years that lay immediately ahead. And when in due course the 'rabble' did sweep them from their positions, and closed the waters of far-reaching change above their heads, they struggled to the surface and found a scene which horrified them. They had thought themselves the masters of the storm; but the storm had thrust roughly past them, sweeping them aside. They climbed out on the bank as best they could, and began to plan their come-back.

Their come-back was still far ahead in the years of national resurgence after Nkrumah's appearance on the scene; but they were always important, and it is necessary to understand them. Often they were excellent men. Sometimes, like Danquah, they were men of great distinction. But they were deeply formed by the long years of the colonial period, and they accepted what the colonial period had taught them.

Africans, they thought, should certainly be free to rule themselves, but only with the guidance of men to whom the British had revealed the secrets of British institutions and examples. Half-way up the colonial mountain, safely at rest in privileged positions, they were content with the prospect of being lifted slowly to its summit, while the rest of the population toiled obediently after them, but at a safe and respectful distance. Any other way of getting self-rule, they were convinced, must open the way to 'disorders' in which their own positions would be lost. To throw in their lot with the 'rabble', or to allow the 'rabble' a share in leadership, could only be in their eyes a programme for disaster.

There is a Chinese fable which tells about them very well. Once upon a time there was a good old chief who fell in love with the idea of dragons. He employed artists to make pictures of dragons for the walls of his palace. He called on sculptors to make carvings of dragons. He commissioned potters to make china figures of dragons. He made speeches to all his friends in praise of dragons.

And then, one dreadful day, a real dragon heard about all this love for his kind. This real dragon decided that the good old chief must surely be its friend among men, and dragons are liable to be short of friends, or at any rate of friends in high places. So it swished its tail and went to the chief's palace, and banged on the door with its rough unlovely snout. And when the door was opened it bared its rows of gleaming teeth in what was meant to be a friendly smile, and asked the good old chief to take it in and give it a home in the palace. But the good old chief had the fright of his life. He shouted to his servants to slam the door in the dragon's face and to run for spears, swearing that it was not *this* kind of dragon that he loved.

So it was with the dragon of anti-colonial agitation, in the Gold Coast of 1947 or after, and the good old chiefs of the U.G.C.C. They too had talked endlessly of the beauties of anti-colonial change, and of future days when Africans would rule themselves, free and independent. They had written many books about all that, and made all sorts of speeches on the subject. They had even called home a young American graduate in order to make some more.

But when Nkrumah and the 'rabble' came thumping on the door of power, bringing with them the rough unlovely snout of popular agitation, these gentlemen were as horrified as the chief in the Chinese fable. They tried hard to slam the door. But the dragon on this occasion was too quick for them.

GETTING READY

Things for Nkrumah went quietly at first.

The bosses of the U.G.C.C. welcomed him back and told him to get on with the job. The new Constitution of 1946 had given them a little of what they wanted; they thought that with careful pressure they could now win more.

They provided Nkrumah with the promised motor car, a sad old thing that could still be made to move, and instructed him to open an office. The place chosen for it was a quiet little seaside town called Saltpond. Nkrumah was able to rent part of an aged building that belonged to the great British trading corporation, the United Africa Company.

There was much to do. The new general secretary discovered that the U.G.C.C. had actually formed only two branches, though its records claimed fifteen. Driving round the country, he began to form more. Within six months, he had formed a great many in the coastal districts alone.

Already he was working with the concentration and unceasing vigour that marked him later. 'His capacity for work was enormous,' one of his close collaborators, Michael Dei-Anang, would long afterwards write of him; and

so was his desire for innovation; but the combination of these factors, buttressed by a degree of impatience and a deep longing to have all his tomorrows today, made work under Nkrumah seem like running a non-stop factory. It was not unusual to have him phone call at dead of night, suggesting that a new idea that had just occurred to him might be prepared in the form of a memorandum for discussion at a meeting next day.

Toiling to make a political force of the U.G.C.C., he found his overseas experience useful. He had membership cards printed. These he issued to branch members, and pressed for the payment of party dues. He opened a U.G.C.C. banking account. Money from supporters began to arrive in it.

By December 1947 the office at Saltpond had become something of a 'non-stop factory'. Under Nkrumah's supervision it had also produced a written programme for the U.G.C.C. This called on its members 'to ensure that by all legitimate and constitutional means the control and direction of the Government shall within the shortest possible time pass into the hands of the people and the Chiefs'. It was a formula that could mean several different things; soon it was clear that if Nkrumah and the youngmen thought it meant one of these things, the leaders of the U.G.C.C. were determined that it should mean quite another.

Whatever it meant, the formula went together with a growing organization. The British were annoyed at all this activity, but waited to see if anything would really come out of it. They did not have to wait for long.

In January 1948, pushing ahead, Nkrumah called a meeting of the Working Committee of the U.G.C.C., and told its members what he thought should be done, and how it should be done. They should work, he said, on a national scale; not only in the coastal lands but also in the inland country: in Ashanti and the

Northern Territories which the U.G.C.C. leaders had left largely out of their plans. They should combine the effort and influence of all sorts of other organizations: trade unions, co-operative societies, ex-soldiers' and farmers' and women's associations. They should start a campaign of mass political education. They should mobilize the common people.

Having done all that, he recommended in a working-paper, they should launch a 'second period' of action. This should be marked by 'constant demonstrations throughout the country to test our organizational strength, making use of political crises'. Then, in a 'third period', they should move further. They should convene a constitutional assembly of all the people of the country, and draw up a constitution for self-government or national independence. And in this third period they should go in for 'organized demonstration, boycott and strike—our only weapons to support our pressure for Self-Rule'.

All this was tough and disagreeable language for the respectable gentlemen of the U.G.C.C. But they agreed in principle, having their own reasons for doubting whether anything need come of it. The dragon certainly looked like a dragon, but perhaps it was only made of paper? If it turned out real, they could still slam the door on it; or so they thought.

But then, with a clash of anger and a burst of firing by the police, there came the 'disturbances' of February 1948. Like many events that have moved history, these 'disturbances' were in no way planned: they simply erupted from the ferment of the times. They took the British by surprise. They took everyone by surprise.

Nii Bonne's boycott of European shops, aimed at getting prices down, came into effect on 28 January. It proved very popular. Nii Bonne had found a language that ordinary people could understand. He did not talk about remote and abstract things such as colonialism or liberty; he talked about the cost of living. 'This cloth,' he would say to a crowd in the street, holding up a length of printed cotton made in Manchester or some other city far from Africa, sold by the white man at 84 shillings per piece, and sold at the black market for £6 per piece, cost the white man about 40 shillings landed here in these days.

If the white man sells it at 50 shillings he would gain 10 shillings profit on a piece. If he sells it at 84 shillings he collects a profit more than the print cost him. Is the white man not cunning taking away your money for nothing?

The people will reply, 'Yes, the white man is stealing our money by tricks.' Nii Bonne will then say, 'Don't buy anything from the white man's stores and don't allow your fellow countrymen to buy. If they do, swear the oath of the Omanhene on them . . .'

Nii Bonne knew what he was up to. Swearing the oath of the Omanhene, as was well understood, meant that anyone who 'broke the oath'—in this case, shopped at the white man's shops —could be brought before the Chiefs' Courts for breaking a taboo. So the breakers of the boycott would be breaking the customary law of the country: they, not the boycotters, would be legally at fault.

In any case the boycott worked. Government and importing companies agreed to reduce prices. This reduction was to come into effect on 28 February. But something else came into effect that day, and it was to count for much more.

In Accra that day, down the dusty highway to the old white-walled castle of Christiansborg where the Governor presided, there appeared the careful ranks of a contingent of the Ex-Servicemen's Union of the Gold Coast. They were not many in number, and their march was a peaceful one. None of them had arms. All they meant to do was to make a demonstration in support of grievances of their own, connected with pensions and prospects of work, and to present a petition to the Governor.

At a point on that coastal highway where another short road leads to the castle, by the sea's edge, these ex-servicemen came up against a line of police. The police had rifles. They ordered the procession to halt, and then to continue on the coastal highway so as not to reach the castle. The ex-servicemen were not content with that. Tempers rose. A white police officer seized a rifle from one of his men and opened fire with it. An ex-sergeant among the demonstrators was killed; several others were wounded.

Looking back, it may not seem much in comparison with the tumults of the world today. But the effect then was shattering. Half a mile away and less, the markets of Accra were filled with people pricing goods at European and Syrian stores, so as to find out if the promised price cuts were being made. They were not being made; or so it was believed. Perhaps they were going to be made later. Who knows? With the crackle of rifle fire and the surge of rumours that followed it, people did not stay for an answer. They began attacking the shops, and then they began looting the shops, and then they began burning the shops.

Rioting continued for days, spreading to other towns. By the time it was over many people had lost their lives. Some two million pounds' worth of property had been destroyed. Much more than that had been destroyed. There went up in the smoke of those burning stores the whole great myth of the 'model colony', law-abiding and content, always ready to come to Britain's aid in times of Britain's trouble, ever prepared to be patient and respectful in its everyday behaviour.

The Governor of the Gold Coast Colony and Protectorate in that climactic moment happened to be a man of whom little further would be heard. With others like him, he was about to pass from the scene, forgotten on the sidelines of a history that had no place for him. But in that moment he had to act, and he acted in a way that was soon to be familiar in many other countries of the colonial world.

Appalled at what had happened under his governorship, harried by an angry Colonial Office in London, the Governor listened to his police officials. They, at least, were ready with their answer. Nothing like this had ever happened before. Why had it happened now? Not, they assured him, because of any shortcomings in the administration, not for any reasons internal to the country. The disaster, they held, was the work of a conspiracy; in fact, of a communist plot. Arrest the leading plotters, and all would again be well. So the 'big six' of the U.G.C.C. were duly arrested. These were J. B. Danquah, Eric Akufo Ado, William Ofori Atta, Ako Adjei, Obetsebi Lamptey and Kwame Nkrumah.

The police, of course, were absurdly wrong. None of the 'big six' had the least connection with the ex-servicemen's demonstration, much less with the rioting that followed on the shooting by the police. The Ex-Servicemen's Union was not even part of the U.G.C.C. Aside from this the attitudes of the 'big six' were completely hostile to any violent action, and, apart from Nkrumah, had no more sympathy with 'communism' than the Governor himself. Together with Nii Bonne and the chiefs who had supported the boycott, they were horrified by rioting which, they judged, could only be a major setback to their plans. But the Governor, and government in London, preferred to think otherwise. What else but 'subversive foreign agitation' could have thus destroyed the obedient calm of the Gold Coast? They would at once appoint a commission of inquiry, and the commission would undoubtedly drag a communist plot into the light of day.

Led by the late A. A. Watson, K.C., a commission was appointed. It entirely failed to find a communist plot, though not for want of trying. It examined a mass of papers collected by the police. Among these was the 'constitution' of the Circle chaired by Nkrumah while in London, and this document, as we have seen, was taken as dire confirmation of Nkrumah's 'foreign connections' of a Soviet Russian and therefore communist sort. Thus encouraged, the commission went on to find that Nkrumah's working-paper for the U.G.C.C., drawn up a few months earlier, was the kind of programme that 'is all too familiar to those who have studied the technique of countries which have fallen the victims of Communist enslavement'.

Even in those fanatical days of the Cold War, when communistic plots were liable to be found under every radical's bed, this was precious thin stuff from which to weave the fabric of

red conspiracy. Released after eight weeks in detention so as
o give evidence to the commission, the 'big six' all denied their
complicity in the 'disturbances'. The commission had to accept
his, because it so manifestly was the truth. Having accepted it,
however, the commission changed the direction of its attack.
t went on to criticize the country's colonial administration.

They were commissioners who had gone through the second
world war, and were aware that much must now change in the
wake of it, here in the Gold Coast as well as at home. They
found the Governor's ideas out-of-date. They discovered 'an
intense suspicion that the chiefs were being used by the Government as an instrument for the delay, if not for the suppression,
of the political aspirations of the people'. The Burns Constitution
of two years earlier, they concluded, 'was outmoded at birth':
the very constitution which, as the Governor still believed, would
be satisfactory and effective for many more years. There would
have to be a new constitution. There would have to be fresh
concessions to African opinion.

While the Governor and officials digested these unwelcome
remarks and prepared to reject them, back at Saltpond Nkrumah
watched and worked. Would the bosses of the U.G.C.C. make
the most of this unexpected opportunity, or would they fall back
on their old tactics of timid pressure for small gains? Was the
time coming near when he would have to break with them?

The leaders of the U.G.C.C. now began to think that they
should break with him. Deeply shaken by their experience, they
were wounded by the accusations of communism and worried
by the signs of popular agitation. It occurred to them that
their general secretary was a nuisance to them, but might also
be a danger. Given the popular fires of enthusiasm he seemed
to be raising everywhere he went, they began to see him in
much the same light as the British now saw him. What kind of
a man was this that they had saddled themselves with? They
sent down to Saltpond a two-man commission, Obetsebi Lamptey
and William Ofori Atta, to go through his files and personal
papers. Some of these they found alarming. Among them were

C

letters in which Nkrumah had used the word 'comrade'. Even the most respectable members of the British Labour Party were accustomed to call each other comrade. But the U.G.C.C. leaders saw it as a plain proof of subversion.

They called him before them. 'Why do you persist in using the word comrade as a term of address?' they asked him. 'Why do you still continue connections with the West African National Secretariat? Why do you welcome the Watson Commission's laying the blame for the disturbances on the Convention [U.G.C.C.]?'

It was not quite enough to justify sacking him, but they suspended him from duty and looked for other grievances. A number of students and teachers had declared a 'sympathy strike' during the detention of the 'big six'. Predictably, the students were expelled from their schools and the teachers were fired. After returning from detention, Nkrumah tried to help them. He hired a little hall in the seaboard town of Cape Coast, not far from Saltpond, for eight shillings a month. Three of the fired teachers agreed to teach the expelled students, and to do this for nothing till funds could be raised. Nkrumah spent ten pounds of his own small salary, then twenty-five pounds a month, to buy packing cases and planks for seats and desks. It was a very small affair, a gesture of solidarity in return for the sympathy strike. Nkrumah called this school—it had only ten students to begin with—the Ghana College, deliberately using a name that should be a political signpost to the future. A year later it had 230 students, and other such 'colleges' were founded.

The U.G.C.C. working committee accused him of exceeding his authority. They made other complaints. Their general secretary had now founded a newspaper of his own, the *Accra Evening News*, primitive in appearance and printed by hand, sometimes by Nkrumah himself, that spoke in the kind of language that common folk could read and understand. Once again the general secretary was getting 'out of hand'. Then there was the Committee on Youth Organization (C.Y.O.) which Nkrumah formed with one of his closest fellow-workers, Kombo Gbedemah,

s chairman. The U.G.C.C. did not like this at all, for the C.Y.O.
roved immediately attractive to the younger men who were now
eginning to take a hand in active politics, who read the *Accra
Evening News*, and who responded to its strong and simple
logans.

These 'youngmen' knew that the U.G.C.C. leaders had no time
or them. But they on their side had no time for the U.G.C.C.
olicy of timid pressure for small gains. They declared in the
C.Y.O. for a policy more radical and urgent. They called for
Self-Government NOW' as distinct from the U.G.C.C.'s 'Self-
Government in the shortest possible time'. On paper, the differ-
nce between the two looks small. Yet it was more than a matter
f words. It was the difference between the calculations of
rivileged persons, and the deep excitement of ordinary people
who sensed that if ever the moment had come to shove aside
he colonial mountain, this was probably it.

In fact, the die was cast. Many things had engraved it with
he aspirations and determination of ordinary people: the sense
f coming change that had followed the second world war, the
pread of elementary education, the anger at low living standards
n the towns, and, swelling with an irresistible hope, the longing
o be free. All these made the real difference that stood between
he masses and the 'men of substance' of the U.G.C.C.

Yet every great change, growing in the hearts and minds of
men, needs its crucial instrument of leadership. This was pro-
ided by Kwame Nkrumah; and it is in this vital sense that
Nkrumah shaped the course of history. When the break came, in
uly 1949, he was ready for it.

ANXIOUS DAYS

n June 1949 the youngmen and their leaders, gathered in a
meeting of the C.Y.O. at Tarkwa, faced the question of what
o do next.

There were in fact two questions. Should they accept
Nkrumah's dismissal from the secretaryship of the U.G.C.C.?

They decided to resist it, at least for the time being. Secondly
should they stay in the U.G.C.C., or break away into a move
ment of their own? On this, opinions differed; the debate wen
on far into the night. Some were for keeping the C.Y.O. insid
the U.G.C.C. because, they argued, this would give the C.Y.O.
chance of leading the U.G.C.C. instead of, as now, being le
by it. Others, more experienced in political work, urged
complete break.

Those who spoke for this second opinion included Koj
Botsio and Komlo Gbedemah. Asked his own opinion, Nkruma
came down heavily for a break. Without it, he argued, the C.Y.O
would become a prisoner of the U.G.C.C. At the back of hi
mind, no doubt, were those anxious discussions in London tw
years earlier: to serve the U.G.C.C. or not, and if to serve it
then for how long? 'It might be our beginning, but it could als
be our end.' Then he had not been sure; now he was.

So the youngmen and their leaders broke with the U.G.C.C
and formed a new party. They called it the Convention People'
Party (C.P.P.) 'in order to carry the masses with us', as Nkruma
wrote later, since the masses, by this time, associated activ
politics with the Convention of the United Gold Coast.

They drew up a six-point programme which began by insistin
that their new party would 'fight relentlessly by all constitutiona
means for the achievement of full Self-Government NOW, fo
the chiefs and people of the Gold Coast'. But once again it wa
not the words on paper that counted. These were moderate an
flexible, and might have been made to mean several contradictor
things. What counted was that the youngmen, all those outsid
the 'political class', had found a leadership that would try t
lead them forward. It was Nkrumah's great contribution tha
he knew how to meet this need in a time of doubt and confusion

The first test came on 12 June 1949, when a meeting of man
thousands of people gathered at Saltpond in tense excitemen
to celebrate the formation of the C.P.P. Waves of cheerin
thundered for the appearance on the platform of every speaker
loudest of all for Nkrumah himself. Would he stand fast? How

vould things go then? The colonial mountain was still tall and
owering above them. Its rocks of wrath could still come
crashing down upon their heads. Many who were there that day
must have feared the outcome. Their cheering had the edge of
sharpness that comes at such a moment.

Nkrumah's months of experience at meetings large and small,
during the past two years, helped him now. He knew that
ordinary people fixed on doing something difficult demand
serious argument. He gave it to them. He reviewed the political
situation in Britain. He argued that Britain's Labour Government would be more likely to listen to their demands than a
Conservative Government, and that it would be wise to act
while a Labour Government was still in power. He spoke
against adopting 'backstairs' methods of pressure, such as the
leaders of the U.G.C.C. preferred, telling the crowd that the
British would better respect 'frankness and firmness'. He insisted
that only a policy of no compromise on the question of self-
government could have any chance of success. He affirmed that
such a chance, if pushed for now, was there to be taken. They
listened and approved.

Then he switched his tone, striking an emotional note. Only
unity could bring them success. Would they follow him if he
led? Or should he pack his things 'and leave this dear Ghana
of ours'? And when the answering shouts came back, that he
should not, he asked again: 'May I remain here and keep my
mouth shut?' And when the voice of that enormous crowd bade
him to 'stay and open your mouth', he took together with them
the step that they were waiting for. He announced that the
C.Y.O. would 'transform itself into a fully-fledged political party
with the object of promoting the fight for Self-Government NOW'.

The thousands at Saltpond separated and went their ways,
returning to their towns and villages, telling of what they knew.
Months of furious activity came next, not only in the coastal
country but also far northward into the forests of Ashanti, and
beyond them in the plains of the north where, until now,
nobody had spoken of modern politics, the politics of national-

ism. The nation of Ghana was not yet born. But these were the months of its conception.

That is what one can see now. It was far more difficult to see it at the time. Many did not see it at all. Nkrumah had formed a new party, a party of no compromise. But he was still general secretary of the U.G.C.C.; or wasn't he? No one could be quite sure; he wasn't even sure himself. He was riding the dragon of popular enthusiasm; but the dragon was also giving signs of being difficult to steer.

Colonial power, meanwhile, was quite intact. Nearly all the important chiefs, as well as almost all the lawyers and business-men of the 'political class', were running for cover, faced as they felt themselves to be, in the words of one of them, by a coalition of 'verandah boys, hooligans, flotsam and jetsam, town rabble'. Nkrumah hesitated, understanding the challenge, uncertain of the best way to meet it. Perhaps it might be wise, for the moment, to temporize with the U.G.C.C.?

There followed incidents of a prophetic nature, revealing much that would happen after the C.P.P. had taken office. The working committee of the U.G.C.C. appointed arbitrators to settle their dispute with Nkrumah. These recommended his reinstatement as general secretary, and that the newly formed C.P.P. should work 'as a vanguard' inside the U.G.C.C. Perhaps sure of what would happen, Nkrumah accepted. With their bluff called, the working committee shied away. Except for his old timber-merchant friend, George Grant, they resigned to a man.

Another confrontation followed. New arbitrators proposed that Nkrumah be reinstated as general secretary and the C.P.P. dissolved. Again Nkrumah accepted, but made it a condition of his acceptance that the delegates present at the meeting should elect a new committee, and that this new committee should work out, with him, policies for a reformed U.G.C.C. Ordinary people might be disappointed, even angry, but the British might also be more likely to listen to a party which, at least in appearance, had the backing of the 'political class'.

There was in fact no ground for any such compromise. The

leaders of the U.G.C.C. must have closed with his offer, if they had been politically less foolish, and used the resulting situation as a means of restoring their political credit. It seems likely that he saw this danger, and that he reckoned with their foolishness. It enabled him, safely enough, to provide the British with a proof that he could be 'reasonable' if his demands were met. The British had yet to learn this. For them, Nkrumah was still one of the 'wild men' with whom they could not deal.

He was in any case saved from the danger of U.G.C.C. acceptance. No sooner had the delegates present at the meeting passed a vote of no confidence in the members of the old working committee, thus announcing that they were ready for a reformed U.G.C.C., than a message came into the conference room from a crowd outside the door. They called for Nkrumah and shouted that he should resign.

He says in his autobiography that he at once made up his mind, and went back into the room with his resignation. This is what actually happened, but whether it tells the whole truth of the incident is another question. Was the call to resign pre-arranged, just in case the working committee went along with him? The autobiography was written and published in 1957 at a moment when Nkrumah wished above all to appear as a 'reasonable' man. Its testimony tends to be discreet on incidents such as this one.

The break was now complete. There could be no further talk of compromise with the 'political class'. Either the C.P.P. would make good its struggle for independence, or the C.P.P. would be destroyed by failure, and Nkrumah and his colleagues along with the C.P.P. Which it was to be, given the pace of events, could not be long in doubt.

COMING TO GRIPS

At once the conflict sharpened. In October 1949 there appeared the report of a commission appointed to inquire into what action should be taken, if any, on the recommendations of the

Watson commission, the body which had inquired into the disturbances of February 1948, and in so doing had called for political reform. This new commission was an all-African affair presided over by Mr Justice Coussey. Its report gave the signal for a fresh surge of nationalism, though this was not its intention; and it will be well to see why.

The Watson commission of 1948, composed of Englishmen who knew little or nothing of Africa, had certainly condemned Nkrumah and his colleagues. But it had also poured a lot of scorn on the colonial administration of the country. This administration, its members said, was out of tune with the times, tending to rely on outworn ideas and institutions. Among these institutions the commission singled out the chiefs for particular criticism. The commissioners could not see that the chiefs had any further useful role to play. The chiefs, they implied, were a hangover from the unregenerate past.

All this had vastly angered government and chiefs alike. Who were these ignorant men from London to tell them how they should behave? Government saw to it that the next commission should consist of Africans, but of Africans who were well aware of the importance of chiefs. This new commission was Mr Justice Coussey's.

The Coussey constitutional committee, as it was more accurately called, went to work, consulting a great many people but none of the leaders of the C.P.P. Its October report recommended a bigger legislature with more elected Africans, the appointment by the Governor of African ministers to his Executive Committee, and other advances on the constitution of three years earlier. But it did not recommend self-government. And it gave a large place to the chiefs who, it proposed, should be endowed with the right to choose one-third of the members of the new legislative assembly. In due course London accepted this report, but improved still further the position of the chiefs.

The advances were considerable. There was to be a National Assembly with seventy-five African members, and there were to be eight African ministers on the Governor's Executive. But the position given to the chiefs ensured its rejection by the C.P.P., just as it guaranteed U.G.C.C. acceptance. The chiefs were to be in a position to choose thirty-seven of these members, while another thirty-three were to be elected indirectly, by 'electoral colleges' in which the chiefs would also have a say. Only five members were to sit in the Assembly by direct election of the popular vote.

As well as these there were to be two appointed Europeans (one for the Chamber of Mines and the other for the Chamber of Commerce), and three British officials nominated by the Governor. Even if the C.P.P. were to win all the seats contested by the popular vote, and all those allocated by votes in 'electoral colleges', they would still be in a minority. The majority would stay with the representatives of the chiefs and the colonial power, so long as these stuck together; and stick together was what they would surely do.

The leaders of the C.P.P. knew very well that it was in their interest to carry with them as many chiefs as they could. But they could not accept this report, and they at once denounced it. In November Nkrumah organized a vast gathering in Accra, naming it the Ghana People's Representative Assembly, and formalized their opposition. London, it resolved, must realize that the Coussey recommendations were unacceptable. The meeting went on to call for 'immediate self-government, that is, for full Dominion status within the Commonwealth of Nations': for an independent status, in other words, equal to that enjoyed by the 'old white Dominions' such as Canada, New Zealand, and South Africa, and now by the new Asian Dominions of India and Ceylon. The whole works, in short, and nothing less.

This made good the promise of the great June meeting at Saltpond which had launched the C.P.P., and it met with a wide support outside the 'political class'. But how to put teeth into this demand? Now, if ever, was the time for the 'third period' of direct action, the period of what Nkrumah had also called 'positive action'. Positive Action became the slogan of the day.

Nkrumah was convinced that Positive Action must be nonviolent. Anything else, he thought, would play into the hands of colonial power. In December he wrote an article in the *Evening News*, entitled 'The Era of Positive Action Draws Nigh', announcing that Positive Action would begin, on a date chosen but not revealed, if the British within two weeks had not accepted the C.P.P.'s demand for a constituent assembly. But there must be no violence.

This was in line with his own beliefs. But it was also in line with the situation as it then appeared. Such was the all-powerful strength of colonial rule, unbroken anywhere in Africa, that any challenge by violence seemed certain to the leaders of the C.P.P., as well as to pretty well everyone else, to end in defeat.

If Nkrumah had no doubt about this, nor did the Governor and his advisers. They were entirely confident that a trial of force would leave them the winners. So sure were they of this that they now embarked on some violent action of their own. This duly confirmed that the losers were to be those who *began* the violence. For the Governor's trial of force was precisely what hastened his undoing.

He seized the dragon by the tail, and that was not difficult. But to cage the creature was another matter. The Governor and his advisers also had their difficulties. One needs to understand these, too. To begin with, there was no good excuse for a policy of repression. No new disturbances had occurred, no new troubles had broken out. Another kind of colonial administration might still have simply set its police to work, arrested whomever they wished, and got away with it. That is exactly how the French governor of the neighbouring Ivory Coast was then acting against Ivory Coast nationalism. Years later, the Portuguese police would cram their colonial prisons with suspects long before any violence had broken out, and shoot without mercy into defence-less crowds.

But the British in the Gold Coast could not do anything like this for two reasons. In the first place, it was against their practice and tradition there. They had governed the Gold Coast on the basic policy that one day the Africans would rule themselves. That day might be thought of as very distant, but the idea was present in the background; and it had led over the years to a sort of partnership-in-prospect between the Governors, who ruled as dictators, and the 'political class' who were believed to speak for African opinion.

There was another reason why the British in the Gold Coast could not easily resort to mass repression. This was that the Governor, however autocratic and complete his powers might be, was answerable to the British Government, and the British Government in turn to the British Parliament. Now the British Parliament in 1949 still had a Labour majority, and the Government was therefore a Labour Government. In terms of decolonization this government was certainly a cautious one, ever troubled by fears of 'communism', distrusting of Africans, eager to make haste as slowly as it could. For all that, it was a government open to considerable internal pressure from groups and persons in the Labour Party who saw it as a duty to dismantle the bastions of Britain's imperial system. Labour had done this in India, however confusedly, and they were ready at least in principle to do it in Africa. If with reservations, they were in favour of decolonization and they were against policies of repression.

This 'metropolitan factor' in British colonial Africa was not without its influence on colonial policies, and Nkrumah was well aware of its possible influence. He knew that an African recourse to violence would not only bring down the furies of colonial repression, but would justify that repression in the eyes of the very people in London who were most likely to favour the long-term demands of the C.P.P. So he had to fight his battle on several fronts; and he had to be careful of the choice of weapons.

As it was, events soon passed beyond his control. Even before he rather nervously launched Positive Action at a public meeting on 8 January 1950, the trade unions had declared for a general strike. Their call to action was widely followed in the urban centres, especially in Sekondi-Takoradi. The people had now seized the initiative, and the strike widened. Public services, such as they were, began to grind to a halt. Trade began to dry up as worried shopkeepers closed their stores.

But did the people mean to keep the initiative? It was not so sure. As the government multiplied its warnings and moved into the manning of trains and buses by strike-breakers recruited for the purpose, Positive Action seemed to falter, at least in Accra where it greatly mattered. Nkrumah was disturbed. The moment was an anxious one.

He need not have worried. The Governor had wished to negotiate with him so as to get him to call off Positive Action. But the talks led nowhere: as the British saw it, the 'wild men' of the C.P.P. had taken over, and only a trial of strength would bring them to heel. On 11 January, accordingly, the Governor declared a state of emergency. Arrests began and multiplied. Police raids became a familiar sight. Another ex-servicemen's demonstration collided with the police; this time two policemen, both Africans, were killed. The repression grew stronger. It was still a very moderate repression, as such things go, and accepted in London as right and proper. For a while it seemed that this might be enough.

But the Governor misread the forces in play. Unless he were to maintain the repression for a long while, and stiffen it, this was the time when he needed, above all, to secure agreement with the leaders of the people. Instead of doing that, he arrested them. On 21 January the police hauled in most of the well-known men of the C.P.P. On the next day they seized Nkrumah.

Now it was deadlock, but greatly to the Governor's disadvantage. The Governor had locked up the only persons to whom the mass of ordinary folk would listen; now he had to explain to London what he had done, and what he was going to do next. The nationalists, whether crowded into prisons or not, had nothing to explain. Popular before, now they were heroes. Like the Governor, the nationalists also wondered what they should do next. But in this they had the edge, for it was the Governor who had to act first.

BREAK-THROUGH

The Governor had to act first, and it was difficult for him. He was a new man on the scene, and, though shrewder than his predecessor, he found his dilemma a tough one. Police repression might be a temporary solution; indulged in too long, or too ferociously, it could only widen the gulf between the British and their 'subjects'.

For the moment, the mood in Accra was one of worried expectation. Tucked away behind their bars, Nkrumah and his fellow-leaders of the C.P.P. had no pleasant holiday. They were treated at first as common law criminals instead of political prisoners, and seemed likely to remain in their cells for quite a while. But what would happen if they did so remain?

The Governor moved cautiously. The British in their colonies had always believed in allowing time, whenever possible, to solve their problems for them. Perhaps time would do the job again? To begin with, it looked that way. Things quietened down. The star of the C.P.P. seemed once more on the wane. Little by little the new Governor, Sir Charles Arden-Clarke, lifted the emergency regulations, called off the police, gave time its chance to take effect. Meanwhile he went ahead with preparations for municipal elections scheduled to be held in three important towns, Accra, Kumasi, and Cape Coast. Perhaps something could still be made of the respectable men of the U.G.C.C.? The elections would give these a chance to recover the lead they had lost in 1949, and the timid gains of the Coussey proposals would then be accepted as enough. Then the Gold Coast would move towards an eventual political independence, but in the time of Britain's choosing, still far ahead, and under the lead of men who could be relied upon to be 'good boys'.

In fact the calm was only on the surface. The well-informed weekly, *West Africa*, might describe the campaign of Positive Action as 'a damp squib', and point out on 28 January that the general strike 'was clearly broken after twelve days'. But two weeks later the same journal could also report that the mood was not one of defeat, but of anger. 'Workers in Sekondi-Takoradi, especially railway employees, show bewilderment and resentment at the failure of "positive action".' And this 'resentment among railwaymen in Sekondi-Takoradi is increased by the detaining in custody of Mr Pobee Biney, railway union president and vice-president of the T.U.C. [Trades Union Congress of the Gold Coast], and Mr Anthony Woode, acting secretary of the T.U.C.'.

On 18 February Woode was sentenced to a year's imprisonment 'for provoking an illegal general strike', and Pobee Biney to eight months on the same charge. The law was 'taking its course'. But so was the resentment.

Imprisonment had not deprived the C.P.P. of skilful leadership. One of its best organizers had come out of prison just as Nkrumah and others were going in. This was Komlo Gbedemah, who had completed an eight months' sentence for libel and sedition, and was now set free. He vigorously took over the acting chairmanship of the C.P.P., kept its newspapers going, and saw to it that work was put in hand to win the municipal elections, as well as any other elections that might follow.

In all of these elections of 1950 the C.P.P. proved victorious. Blow after blow, the work of 1949 was confirmed. What the mass of the people wanted was self-government; no further delays were going to shoehorn the U.G.C.C. and the 'political class' back into their favour. From now on there was only one way to break the deadlock. Summing up all that at the end of 1950, *West Africa* commented that 'Mr Nkrumah, whether you agree with him or not, is much the most capable leader of the party, and is the most popular individual in the Gold Coast. Clearly, if he remains in gaol, the new government [to emerge from the elections projected for February 1951] will be like Hamlet without the prince . . .'*

Having put the C.P.P. leaders in gaol, the Governor had somehow to get them out again. But how he would do it was

* Issue of 23 December 1950.

not yet evident. It was Nkrumah, with Gbedemah's aid, who solved the problem. Sitting in prison, he was for some time unsure how best to act. A general election for the legislature was to be held in February 1951. Should he become a candidate, even if he were still in prison? It might be the means of getting his release two years before his three-year sentence was completed; it might also be a political mistake.

Communing with himself, he decided to stand. To do that, however, he had first to get his name on the electoral register. The law said that prisoners sentenced to more than one year's imprisonment were debarred from enrolment on the register. True enough: but his own sentence, he now recalled, was of three terms of one year each. So he could be enrolled. It cost a deal of argument to have this accepted. But it had to be accepted, for it was indeed the law.*

Once enrolled, he was entitled to be a candidate, even if in prison. Some of his friends outside were against this, fearing that he would be disqualified if elected, and that the C.P.P. might thus lose a seat which they could win and keep with another candidate. But Nkrumah's candidature was maintained. He was to stand for Accra Central, the most prominent seat in the country. Gbedemah, its candidate, switched to Keta.

There came fresh weeks of driving political activity. The elections of February 1951 were held on the 8th of that month. Their results were a rolling triumph. At first in the rural areas, and then in the towns, they brought a landslide to the C.P.P. in a festival of red-white-green party flags, eager canvassers, excited voters, countless rallies and demonstrations. Positive Action might have failed in any direct sense; indirectly, through the ballot box, it totally carried the day.

Nothing like this had been thinkable before. Even as prominent a chief as Sir Tsibu Darku, veritable monument of the 'political class', was defeated by the engine driver, Pobee Biney, who had lately gone to prison for his part in the January strike. And at Accra Central, with Nkrumah as candidate, the landslide was

* Had government foreseen this contingency? No one has yet claimed this.

complete. Accra Central polled 23,122 votes. Its C.P.P. candidate in gaol received 22,780 of them. It was total, undeniable, irreversible success.

Bowing to it, Governor Arden-Clarke released the C.P.P. men five days later. Defending his decision to a critical British audience some years later, he recalled that:

Nkrumah and his party had the mass of the people behind them . . Without Nkrumah, the [new] Constitution would be still-born, and if nothing came of all the hopes, aspirations and concrete proposals for a greater measure of self-government, there would no longer be any faith in the good intentions of the British Government . . . the Gold Coast would be plunged into disorders, violence and bloodshed.*

Nkrumah had one hour's notice of his release. But Gbedemah made sure that many others had almost as much. When the prison gates clanged shut behind him as he stepped into the street, Nkrumah found himself in a struggling tumult of joyful voters. They carried him in triumph to the West End Arena of Accra, the meeting-place of the Ghana People's Representative Assembly, the place that the C.P.P. had made especially its own. There they sacrificed a sheep, as ancient custom provided, and caused him to step seven times in its blood so as to be ritually cleansed from the stains of prison.

The next day the Governor invited him to Christiansborg Castle. It was very much the British way. If it was necessary to talk to Nkrumah, since there was no one else worth talking to, there would be no stinting of the red carpet. The British would greatly have preferred to negotiate with the 'good boys' of the U.G.C.C., but these were powerless. Like it or not, they would

* *African Affairs*, Journal of the Royal Africa Society, London, January 1958. Mr David Williams has recalled for me that 'the Colonial Office knew that Nkrumah would win and, in the person of Sir Andrew Cohen, had decided that he must be released as soon as the election was over in order to lead the government. Arden-Clarke told me that he could not release Nkrumah before the election, although he would have liked to do that, because the opposition [U.G.C.C.], already doomed to defeat, would have then alleged that the British had brought about their defeat.'

negotiate with Nkrumah. The whole question was: could they negotiate with him? Would he prove 'sensible', this man of fiery reputation and 'communist' associations?

Arden-Clarke had his doubts on the subject, but he also had no option. He made the best of it. Big and easy-going, knowing much of Africa and feeling at home among Africans, he had no personal aversion to welcoming yesterday's prisoner—the 'prison graduate' as his followers now called him—to the castle of imperial power. It was not the first time that a British colonial governor had opened the prison gates on a nationalist leader one day, and shaken hands with him the next; and it would by no means be the last. One after another, in the years that followed on the triumph of the C.P.P. in the Gold Coast, Africa's leaders would leave prison for the seats of power.

Nkrumah nursed no bitterness. He came to the castle in an hour of triumph, but more than ready to show that the victor could rise above the feelings of the persecuted. He came with the roar of joyful crowds ringing in his ears. Now, at last, the colonial mountain could be shoved aside. It might still need a huge effort; at least the effort would begin today.

They had never met before. Now they met warily, probing each other's positions. Always a good tactician, Nkrumah understood the Governor's dilemma: the Governor held all the power but was obliged to part with some of it. How much? That was Nkrumah's question. On his side, the Governor knew that Nkrumah was the only man in the country whom the mass of people would follow. A deal with Nkrumah and the C.P.P. would give the British a breathing-space, perhaps a long one. How little need he give away? That was his question.

They talked, and the early tensions of their meeting gradually relaxed. The man from prison and the man of imperial majesty had expected to dislike each other. But now, face to face, they liked each other almost from the start. Arden-Clarke opened his offer. If Nkrumah and the C.P.P. would play the parliamentary game by Britain's rules, they would meet with no obstacles. If they gave up the claim to self-government now, they could expect self-government soon. Would Nkrumah consult his colleagues and form a government? It would still be a colonial government. The Governor would hold the power that mattered. But it would also be a step, perhaps a long step, towards political independence.

To Nkrumah, listening, it was the old problem over again, the same problem he had faced in London when invited to return to the Gold Coast as the political employee of men whose views he did not share. Would acceptance mean his end, or his beginning? He had hesitated to accept the offer of the U.G.C.C. in 1947, fearing to be trapped in a compromise that would prove too strong for him. Yet it had not proved too strong. On the contrary, it had led to a triumph for the nationalist cause. And now, in 1951, he was called from prison to castle, and the nationalist position was much stronger than before. In 1947 it had barely existed; now it enjoyed mass support. The lesson seemed unanswerable: how could he hesitate to accept it? How could be reject this offer? Who would understand his motives if he did reject it?

He accepted at once. And so it was that Ghana was born, though with anxious years still to go before independence, from a compromise which neither side liked or trusted, but which neither side thought well to reject. Thus welcomed to the palace of power, the dragon of anti-colonial revolution was asked to be a 'sensible' and moderate creature, and to rest content with the slow and tricky workings of reform. It was to be victory at a heavy price.

But that is not the way it seemed at the time. Nkrumah and his fellow-leaders saw the dangers, but they also saw the gains; and the gains, in the colonial Africa of 1951, were impressively large and real. It crossed the minds of none but the merest handful that Nkrumah should refuse them. To have their own men making the pace, the men they trusted: that is what the mass of people wanted. They made it very clear. Outside in the streets, as he left the Castle, they were singing their own

jubilant acceptance, and all Nkrumah's leading followers were
singing it with them:

> There is victory for us
> In the struggle of the C.P.P.
> There is vic-tor-y for us . . .

3. Towards Independence

Seek ye first the political kingdom . . .
Kwame Nkrumah

THE NECESSARY PRICE

This achievement of 1951, partial though it was, gave Nkrumah what was perhaps his greatest hour. Later there would be more obvious advances and more imposing moments of success. But this one, secured when the day of black resurgence had barely dawned along the colonial skyline, surely marked its sunrise. *There is victory for us* . . . The message broke the continental silence like a trumpet blast.

He had done what few thought possible, and opened a breach into the fortress of power where fewer still had looked for any great success. The news of this went out through Africa in electrifying ripples of encouragement to all who hoped for anti-colonial change. Soon it was felt in other British colonies, perhaps most of all in Nigeria, that Nkrumah's breakthrough to internal self-rule could mean a quickened pace for them as well; and what it could mean for them it could also mean, if distantly, for non-British colonies.

Naïvely, long afterwards, some critics would say that Nkrumah and the C.P.P. had simply 'bought the British plan', and that, by accepting a process of slow reform, they had sacrificed the hopes of revolution. These critics were mis-reading history and its possibilities. There was no chance in 1951 of any far-reaching change, much less of revolution. This was partly because of the strength of the whole imperial position. But it was also, and even more, because of the nature of the C.P.P. and the 'general situation' in which it had to operate. Though an assembly of genuine nationalists, the C.P.P. was in no sense a revolutionary party; nor, in the circumstances of that time, could it have been one. Like other such parties or movements in the campaigns for political decolonization during the 1950s, the C.P.P. had neither the experience nor the leadership, much less the 'general situation', that could have carried it beyond a fight for immediate gains.

As it was, the immediate gains were considerable. For if the British had a plan, it was a plan designed to hand over power, as slowly as possible, to the 'political class' in whom they had long seen their prospective junior partners. Now they were obliged to embark on a process of handing over power to men who were not content to remain subordinate; and the difference for Ghana, as well as implicitly for the whole of Africa, was to be a crucial one.

They were not, true enough, handing over power as yet, and Nkrumah suffered from no illusions on the subject. Though in some ways characteristic of the 'populist' leaders of those years, men for whom the fact or promise of immediate gains went far to satisfy ambition and confuse judgement, he was also different from them. He never for a moment forgot the long-term gains on which he had set his heart. He knew that he had forced a breach for further progress, but he also knew that the breach would be worth nothing unless it were radically widened.

He was to form a C.P.P. government in a country still under stiff colonial rule. As the head of this government he was not even to be called prime minister, but only 'leader of government business'. He and his African ministerial colleagues were to have no power in vital questions of foreign policy, national defence, internal security. They were not even to have any power over appointments in the civil service. This power was to be reserved to a 'public service commission' which the British authorities would continue to control. And when they were faced with the demand for fresh concessions, he knew that these authorities would do their best to drag their feet.

Just how successful the British were going to be in doing this, and how far they could count on Ghanaian help in doing it, remained questions for the future. Nobody then could foretell the full weight of the burden that this uneasy compromise of 1951 was to load upon the shoulders of the new government. But even if Nkrumah and his colleagues could have foretold that, it would almost certainly have changed nothing.

Looking back in after-life, wiser from all the experience of this reformist compromise and its consequences, Nkrumah one day confided to C. L. R. James that perhaps it might have been better to have driven 'straight forward for independence, even if such a course had demanded armed insurrection'. There is nothing to suggest that he considered this at the time. There is likewise nothing to suggest that any substantial body of nationalists would have followed him if he had.

A handful of his old friends soon had the same thought. Early in 1952, for example, I remember one of them, Bankole Awooner-Renner, who had endured thirteen months in a Gold Coast prison for nationalist agitation, remarking to me bitterly that 'the initiative has passed from the hands of the oppressed to the hands of the oppressor'. But Renner and the remnant who thought as he did had no more than a peripheral influence on nationalist opinion.

Nkrumah voiced his own doubts. Speaking at a press conference only one day after leaving prison, he denounced the constitution then in force as 'bogus and fraudulent', since its African ministers would be in office but not in power. If they accepted these ministries, it could be only as a necessary stepping stone to genuine self-rule.

Even so, there would be dangers. 'There is a great risk in accepting office,' he warned party members in a message circulated some days later, 'under this new constitution which still makes us half slaves and half free.' He called for 'vigilance and moral courage' to withstand the temptations of

temporary personal advantage . . . Bribery and corruption, both moral and factual, have eaten into the whole fabric of our society and these must be stamped out if we are to achieve any progress. Our election to the Assembly shows that the public has confidence in the integrity of the Party, and that we will not stoop low to contaminate ourselves with bribery and corruption at the expense of the people.

If Nkrumah had made up his mind to take the risk, so had all his leading colleagues. Reform for them was quite enough; they had no doubt at all that it would suit their interests, and, in suiting their interests, meet any demands that the voters might reasonably put. They made ready to take over the ministerial jobs allotted to them; Kojo Botsio as minister of education and social welfare; Komlo Gbedemah as minister of health and labour; Archie Casely-Hayford as minister of agriculture and national resources; Tommy Hutton-Mills as minister of commerce, industry and trade; Ansah Koi as minister of communications and works; and others in lesser posts. They were fired with a determination to show that Africans could rule themselves. They were sure that they could do it.

And the true content of this political achievement, risky compromise though it also was, became at once revealed by the reactions of the 'political class', the 'men of substance' who had assumed, for so long, that the British would ensure their continued supremacy. They had expected something quite different. They had rightly thought the Coussey constitution tailored to their needs. Were they not Britain's true friends, the spokesmen of 'responsible opinion', the representatives of traditional power and influence? Must they now stand by and watch the 'rabble' as it swarmed into the seats of power that Britain had reserved for them? They were angry and disgusted. The British, they cried, had betrayed them.

Said Dr Danquah, moving spirit of the U.G.C.C.: 'Ruthlessly, he [Nkrumah] split the national front, then made a filthy deal with the British . . . One day he said he wanted national freedom, and the next day he compromised with the British . . .' Dr Kofi Busia and other leading lights of the now extinct U.G.C.C. said the same. Eager themselves to accept any compromise the British might have offered them, they found themselves outmanoeuvred, overtaken, left behind. They never forgave Nkrumah.

Several of them, through all the years that followed, were to devote their energy not to building the new State, but to undermining its chances of ever being built at all.

Yet in those early weeks and months it seemed to matter little what they might say or do. U.G.C.C. men such as Francis Awooner-Williams might console themselves by scornful comparisons between 'the men of education and substance, merchant princes working in the interests of the country', and 'the flotsam and jetsam and the popinjays' who had now left them high and dry on the political beach. The fact remained that the merchant princes had completely lost the tide: in some words let fall by Nkrumah at the time, the chiefs had run away and left their sandals behind. Others would now wear the sandals of authority. These others had just achieved far more by two years of popular agitation than the 'men of substance' had gained by thirty years of stately argument and courteous debate.

For a while, little or nothing was heard from the opposition but lamentation and complaint. Nkrumah made it more difficult for them by a careful policy of reconciliation. He disliked and distrusted the chiefs, merchants and men of education; but the chiefs, at least, he feared for the traditional influence they could wield, and above all he feared the influence of the Asantehene or king of Ashanti, the greatest and wealthiest of them all. One of his first actions surprised the opposition. A most eminent representative of the 'men of substance' was chosen as Speaker of the new Legislative Assembly.

It took a little time for these influential men of the established opposition to regain their confidence, and become an effective brake on progress. The general atmosphere, for the moment, was one of happiness and hope.

MEMORABLE DAYS

Looking back, there were occasions then that still glow in the mind. They evoke the atmosphere of extraordinary excitement in which a people's destiny unfolds. Frail though it is, the ship of national independence has seized the tide and squared its sails. And the wind blows well.

Only twelve days elapse between the release from James Fort of the leaders of the C.P.P. and their formal meeting in the Legislature. There they take the oath of allegiance and prepare to start their work. Proudly, they are still wearing their white 'prison graduate' caps. One of the few among them who has not come from prison, Archie Casely-Hayford, the gentle and immensely loyal lawyer of Accra who has stood by them while they were in gaol, is wearing a special one of his own. It is labelled 'D V B': 'Defender of the Verandah Boys', another gesture of popular defiance.

Now the 'verandah boys' are in office, and can show what the common man will do. 'From now on,' observes Nkrumah's old friend, the West Indian George Padmore, also present in Accra, 'it is the plebeian masses, the urban workers, artisans, petty traders, market women and fishermen, the clerks, the junior teachers, and the vast farming communities of the rural areas who are the makers of Gold Coast history'. But they will be generous to their opponents. They choose as their Speaker Sir Emmanuel Quist; he is one of the pillars of the 'political class'. They appeal for national unity. They ask for everyone's support and presence.

On 7 April 1951, after days of frantic preparation, the new Assembly gathers to begin its parliamentary labours. It is another day fraught with tremendous hopes and fears, solemn in its dignity, alive with the thrill of countless meetings up and down the country, of cheers and crowds and future purposes.

Outside the assembly hall, its doors and windows open to the sunlight of the West African seaboard, rather as though it were an assembly aware of acting in the presence of a whole people, there is drawn up a company of the Royal West African Frontier Force. Its regimental colours are flying and its bugles blaring forth. That is important, too. The soldiers of the Gold Coast, of the Ghana now being born, have also played their part.

On many fields of battle they have already fought imperialism in Africa. They it was, the men of the 24th Gold Coast Brigade, together with comrades-in-arms of the 23rd Nigerian Brigade, who stormed the hills and rivers of Ethiopia against the Italian Fascist occupiers of that country, who crossed the Juba river in the face of bitter opposition, and who chased the fleeing Fascists as far as distant Harrar and beyond. And at Wadara, perhaps the toughest of all those East African battles, it was the Gold Coast Brigade that stood virtually alone, save for the help of some Ethiopian irregulars. They had carried the day, and then, afterwards, they had come home and marched in the front ranks of nationalism. Their serving comrades are there today in pomp and splendour, and they have every nationalist right to a place in this resplendent scene.

The assembly hall itself is a small one, always in the past a mere talking-shop for the governor's 'political class', and furnished with a dozen long benches ranged in tiers on either side of a central carpet. It is all a distant echo of the House of Commons, with the Speaker's chair at one end of the carpet and a little visitors' gallery at the other. The atmosphere is duly ceremonial, and an oil painting of the Monarch of Britain is there to make the point.

Sitting in the visitors' gallery are some of Nkrumah's old friends from oversea, marking the presence of the world. They and a handful of journalists are almost in the body of the hall, can almost feel themselves to be part of the proceedings, giving them the sense that Africa's long isolation is at last coming to an end. They lean forward, excited. The newly elected members file in and take their seats, rustling papers, adjusting robes. Then the C.P.P. ministers enter with Nkrumah himself, tense and slender in his cloth.

Next arrives the Governor, Sir Charles Arden-Clarke, the first colonial governor who has ever presided over an assembly such as this. Genial and yet imposing, he is wearing all the majesty of his white uniform and medals, and his tall helmet with plumes. He has come to the door of the assembly with the familiar guard of honour, mounted troopers of the north wearing blue and white turbans, carrying lances. They are the Governor's men, the men of empire; but they stay outside and soon their loyalty must change. Much else will change. It is still hard to believe.

All stand and take their seats again. The proceedings can begin. A new Africa will move into history.

Nkrumah rises. There is a silence around him. It is a hush so deep, for this brief moment, that all the world might be listening. He speaks into this silence, a quiet voice sometimes difficult to hear. It carries the force and travail of the future.

HARSH REALITY

With Nkrumah at their head, the C.P.P. ministers came down to earth from these memorable glories, and went to their desks in the various departments. Even for Nkrumah, who knew what to expect somewhat better than the others, it proved a lowering experience.

The desks were waiting for them, duly cleared and vacated by senior British civil servants who now became their chief assistants and advisers: in the jargon of the civil service, their 'permanent secretaries'. Most of these British officials were studiously polite to their new African bosses; but it was a curious relationship, and it was not an easy one. The lords of yesterday were the servants of today, and yet the British were still in control of the country: the Governor, as before, remained their real master. How far could the new ministers trust in the good will of these colonial officials?

It was hard to know, but there was nothing to be done. The British officials were there, and could not be removed, first of all because they were the Governor's men, and secondly because there were very few Africans, as yet, with enough training for senior administrative jobs. So it was that the C.P.P. had to take over more than an unworkable constitution and a disgruntled opposition, as Nkrumah said afterwards, but also a suspicious civil service:

The Commissioner of Police, for instance, who had won a libel case against me as publisher of the *Evening News*, was still there; the Crown Counsel who so happily led the prosecution at my trial; the Colonial Secretary as Crown witness and hundreds of his colleagues in the government who had taken part in the chase, if not bodily, then certainly in spirit—all these could have been against me.

It was part of the price of the compromise. But Nkrumah soon came to recognize that it was not the biggest part. Most of the British officials served the new government loyally; some of them, duly helped by offers of large monetary 'compensation' for their change of masters, remained in office for years afterwards; a few were genuinely convinced that an African government could make good. At his own level, 'at the top', Nkrumah worked out an easy personal relationship with Arden-Clarke.

The main part of the price paid for this chance of further progress lay elsewhere. It lay in the fact that the new government had to take over where the old left off. It had to take over the laws and institutions of colonial rule, as well as the legacy of the pre-colonial past, with its kings and chiefs and local hierarchies, and do the best with these it could. This meant that the new government had to accept the political and economic structure of the country as it was, and merely try to improve that structure. There could be no question of any major changes in the structure, of any far-going fresh start, of any kind of great renewal. The continuance in office of senior and middle-grade British colonial officials was only an aspect of this inheritance.

What was the country's true position? What were the facts about it? The new ministers had to find out, and they found this far from easy. They had to embark on delicate sessions of questioning with British officials who, not unnaturally, wished to suggest that everything was in splendid order, and that nothing need be done but merely continue as before. They had to spend long hours in probing departmental files whose language and meaning were often hard to interpret, even when, as was sometimes the case, certain files could no longer be 'found' or were still regarded as being fit for British eyes alone.

The measure of their problems gradually became clear to the new ministers. It was only long afterwards, with political independence six years later, that they were able to gain a full understanding; then, as Nkrumah was to say, 'the destitution of the land after long years of colonial rule was brought sharply home to us'. But even in those first months of 1951 the discoveries were clear enough. Colonial rule, it appeared, had simply gone on from one year to the next, content so long as 'law and order' should prevail, disturbed into bursts of sudden activity only when an unusual man such as Guggisberg came on the scene, or when some emergency destroyed the quiet course of their routine.

The Gold Coast had been a relatively favoured colony, largely because of the early colonial exploitation of its capacity to produce cocoa. Yet in those years when the C.P.P. stepped into office 'there were slums and squalor in our towns', Nkrumah was to write in 1964 in one of his challenging books, *Africa Must Unite*,

superstitions and ancient rites in our villages. All over the country, great tracts of open land lay untilled and uninhabited, while nutritional diseases were rife among our people. Our roads were meagre, our railways short. There was much ignorance and few skills. Over 80 per cent of the people were illiterate, and our existing schools were fed on imperialist pap, completely unrelated to our background and our needs. Trade and commerce were controlled, directed and run entirely by Europeans.

There were no mechanical industries save for the extraction and export of gold and diamonds, and a few other minerals. 'We made not a pin, not a handkerchief, not a match. The only cloth we produced was hand-woven *kente*, traditional and exclusive.'* If the country had rich resources under its soil, nothing of these was known to Africans. Geographical surveys had remained confidential to the colonial rulers.

'As a heritage,' he was to recall of independence in 1957, 'it

* *Africa Must Unite*, London, 1963, p. xiii. There was, in fact, a large plywood plant operated by the United Africa Company.

was stark and daunting, and seemed to be summed up in the symbolic bareness which met me and my colleagues when we officially moved into Christiansborg Castle' after independence. 'Making our tour through room after room, we were struck by the general emptiness. Except for an occasional piece of furniture, there was absolutely nothing to indicate that only a few days before people had lived and worked there.' In that fortress vacated by imperial power 'not a rag, not a book was to be found; not a piece of paper; not a single reminder that for many years the colonial administration had had its centre there.'

He might have said the same of 1951, when the C.P.P. took office, except that in 1951 the new ministers knew almost nothing of the problems they must face. But what they centrally found was that the great imperial claim to have 'prepared' the way for African self-rule was nothing but a myth. Out of this there would come great misunderstandings, especially among British and other people who believed the myth. It would be said that Africans had been given the great good fortune of receiving self-rule and independence on a golden dish, polished, shining, and fit for many years of use. The truth was different.

The dish they were handed in 1951, and again in 1957, was old and cracked and little fit for any further use. Worse than that, it was not an empty dish. For it carried the junk and jumble of a century of colonial muddle and 'make do', and this the C.P.P. ministers had to accept along with the dish itself. What shone upon its supposedly golden surface was not the reflection of new ideas and ways of liberation, but the shadow of old ideas and ways of servitude.

In so far as these colonial rulers had 'prepared' the people of Ghana for self-rule and independence—and it can be said for them that they had done more in that direction than any colonial rulers elsewhere—they had done it with the conviction that the new State would continue, like the old, to be a fragment of Britain's sphere of power and influence. They had foreseen a time when the 'chiefs, merchants, and men of substance' would take over the levers of power from the British, and use those

levers as the British had used them. In 1951 there were plenty
of British officials who thought that this could still be made to
happen.

'They are working, as far as one can see, often with self-
forgetting ardour and energy to forward the creation of an
African Dominion of the British Commonwealth,' I noted during
a visit of 1952. 'But—and here is the point—they are working
necessarily within the framework of conservative and capitalist
thinking. The British idea is that the Africans shall fit obediently
into this Commonwealth framework.' It might in those days be
a big advance on the rest of colonial Africa. But there remained
'an overriding question whether such thinking can possibly, in
the nature of things, be compatible with the mental and physical
liberation of a backward country whose development requires
mass efforts and new economic techniques'.

How little it could be compatible was shown during these
years before independence, and again in other years after
independence. The effort to win free from this colonial framework, whether of laws, institutions, or attitudes, became
Nkrumah's daily preoccupation. And this is probably why
Nkrumah also became so deeply resented, and even hated, by
powerful people in Britain and elsewhere. He was not grateful
for the cracked old dish of the colonial framework. He was far
from happy with the junk and jumble that it carried.

On the contrary, he thought and said that the colonialists
should be grateful for being absolved of the sins of colonialism,
and lost few chances of explaining that Africans had suffered
from foreign rule. Then powerful people rounded angrily on this
'good boy' who had turned into a 'bad boy', and poured abuse
upon him. And in doing this, before long, they were joined by
all those 'chiefs, merchants, and men of substance' who thought
themselves defrauded of their 'right' to take and keep the power
for themselves.

Such complaints were few as yet. In 1951 the new ministers
were generally applauded; and the opposition, for a little while,
was silent. Nkrumah and his colleagues informed themselves of

the country's true position; there was little else, in fact, that most of them could do. Then gradually they stepped up pressure for new concessions from the British, and these were agreed. In 1954 they were promised full political independence. In 1957 they achieved it.

Six frustrating years had to pass between the first grand day of victory and the conquest of power. Much, perhaps most, of what afterwards went wrong with Ghana was then given time and room to develop: the price of the compromise of 1951 became ever clearer, and also ever heavier. Yet in history's contradictory way they were fruitful years as well. The C.P.P. in office scored important successes. They faced a great deal of trouble, and overcame it. They met with bitter opposition, and overcame that too. They gave reality to the vision of a liberated Africa.

Little by little they improved the cracked old system of colonial rule, patched it up and polished it, swept it of some of the junk and jumble, added new things of their own. Yet it was still a colonial system, and Nkrumah did not lose sight of the fact. Years later, after independence had opened new opportunities but also sharpened old problems, he was to call it a neo-colonial system. Then he was to try to fashion an entirely new one that could realize the creative possibilities of Africa.

Meanwhile, after 1951, he and his colleagues took stock of their problems. They did not always find the right answers. They made a great many mistakes. But the best of these men also learned from their mistakes. When the years of achievement began to give way to the years of bitterness, after 1961, Ghana was in several important ways a distinctly better country for its people to live in.

But to understand why Nkrumah and the C.P.P. could not accomplish more in those early years, and why those years gave way eventually to bitterness, one needs to see what the real problems were, and why they proved so great a burden.

BLACK MAN'S BURDEN

The problem at the outset was to keep on going towards independence, and make sure there were few diversions. It proved difficult. Having got into office, a number of Nkrumah's colleagues were not long in finding the experience a sufficient one. Even by 1952 the C.P.P. was beginning to be an instrument of patronage, a means of personal livelihood, a stairway to privilege. But the damage was small as yet.

Nkrumah lived these years in a fury of tense and unrelaxing effort. Everyone who knew him has said this, and the fact was obvious, for you found him at work early or late, continually engaged with the business of the moment. Then as after, as Michael Dei-Anang has recalled of the 1960s, his habit was to attend 'to official business with care and concern above the ordinary. He was a stickler for discipline and hated lazy, slip-shod or slovenly work of any kind . . . His working day started long before daybreak . . .' His impatience with delays, his constant struggle for solutions, these were what you remembered of him: these, and his utter personal involvement, his indifference to the flesh-pots, his sense of being indispensable.

Every kind of delay and postponement seemed to get into his path, some raised by Europeans, others by Africans. He collided with these obstacles. He was sometimes stopped by them. More often he thrust them aside. His popularity with the mass of ordinary people remained immense. They crowded to listen to him, named their boy-babies after him, proclaimed their faith in him. It was a time for them when everything seemed possible, even the impossible. Let the new government only lead, and they would press behind.

'What is a National Bank?' I remember early in 1952 a questioner asking at a brains-trust meeting of another symptom of the times, the People's Educational Association.

'The point of this question,' replied the speaker, 'is, I suppose, that we ought to have one of our own?'

If a National Bank was a useful thing that independent

D

nations had, then yes, why not? Wasn't this what independence was about? If the country was not yet independent, was still fast fixed into the Sterling Area, was still the subject of the Bank of England, then all this must be changed tomorrow; or, if not tomorrow, then the day after.

Nkrumah stood at the heart of this whirlwind of expectation. His eyes were on the future, but his feet were still on the ground. He knew what was expected of his government, but he also knew how narrow were its present limits of action. The great need was to expand these limits and achieve the reality of power. Only this would justify the compromise of 1951. But to achieve this he had to ride two horses at the same time. No political leader can find that easy; for Nkrumah it was doubly difficult. The two horses he had to ride were trained to different styles and speeds. Often enough, they were not even going in the same direction.

The first horse was the fiery steed of popular demand for change and progress, a creature best ridden at a gallop, ill-suited to a trot, and hopeless at a walk. The second horse was the comfortable beast of everyday negotiation with the British authorities, and especially with Governor Arden-Clarke; a gentle amble was its only reliable pace, while its head was turned most usually towards its stable and its sack of oats. If the first horse was held back too much it would lose interest in disgust; if the second was spurred it was likely to stop dead in its tracks. Managing this pair became a daily trial of skill.

In a political sense he pinned his hopes to the building of a nation through the unifying influences of a broad parliamentary system of representation. Then, and for years afterwards, he continued to believe that this kind of system would mobilize the active participation of the mass of ordinary people, give them spokesmen they could trust, raise the country's level of political skills and consciousness, and so form the base for the socialist ideas by which alone, as he also continued to believe, Ghana's and Africa's liberation could be realized and kept safe. But even if he had not pinned his hopes to a parliamentary system, there was no other alternative to follow. For the British were determined that the institutions of an independent Ghana should be an amalgam of traditional institutions and of others borrowed from England.

Those who had not forgiven him were still looking round for words that could hurt, and lost no time in finding the word 'dictatorship'. As early as a year within the C.P.P.'s accepting office, I remember an occasion at the house of the late Dr Danquah, heart and soul of the 'political class' who were now in the wilderness, at which this word was hotly thrown around. What Nkrumah wanted, they said, was a C.P.P. dictatorship 'presided over and connived at by the British'. Dr Danquah's chief momentary grievance, I also remember, was the level of income tax; he thought it was too high. If anything, no doubt, it was too low for a country which needed every penny of public funds that it could raise. But even the rate of income tax, at that time, could not sensibly be laid to the fault of Nkrumah and his ministers. They really had no say in the matter.

Much more was to be said about dictatorship. At that time the accusation was merely absurd. As the 'political class' well knew, even if it preferred not to say so, a dictatorship already existed. That was how the British had ruled their colony. Its institutions of authoritarian rule were precisely those that the C.P.P. were obliged to take over. What the C.P.P. were trying to do, as their only hope of achieving independent power as distinct from subordinate office, was to work against these institutions of dictatorship and to build, in their place, a democracy. This was what the 'political class' really held against them: the C.P.P.'s reliance on the support of the 'rabble', of the mass of voters who wanted change and progress. A working democracy, a popular democracy, was the last thing the 'political class' desired: hadn't one of their most prestigious candidates, Sir Tsibu Darku, just lost his election fight to a mere engine-driver?

This anti-democratic attitude of the 'political class' was to work much evil in the years that followed. If the C.P.P. did eventually develop dictatorial ways, the degeneration went hand-in-hand with the irresponsibility of an opposition which refused to play the parliamentary game. This opposition's preference for non-parliamentary and non-democratic manoeuvres was always there: from the earliest times of the national struggle right down to the overthrow of Nkrumah by a military *coup* in which the 'political class' rejoiced. But none of this ever prevented the 'men of substance' from saying that Nkrumah was or wanted to be a dictator, or their foreign friends from saying the same.

The institutions of dictatorship, handed on to the new government by the British, were the true 'black man's burden' in those difficult years. Britain's governor had enjoyed powers that were practically without limit. The Governor, in turn, had ruled through district officers who were 'miniature governors' in the regions where they held sway. They had to obey the laws, but the laws had all been framed to enable them to rule. The whole system rested on the notion that only a few privileged men knew how to govern, and had the power to govern, while the 'dumb mass' must obediently follow. As a means of building an independent nation, it was a system built to guarantee failure.

What Nkrumah and his colleagues first attempted was to bring the administrative machine, the power of the State, within democratic control. For a long while they found this quite impossible; they could not even control the police, let alone the army or the conduct of foreign affairs. All these remained within the colonial system of 'orders from above and obedience from below' with no questions asked, or, at least, no questions answered.

Consider the matter of trade union laws and regulations. No democracy of mass participation can function without representative and effective trade unions. Yet the restrictive Trades Disputes Act, passed in Britain during the 1920s as a means of curbing trade union rights, was still in force in the Gold Coast. None of the new government's British officials, and I asked some of them myself at the time, had any thought of replacing this oppressive piece of legislation by democratic trade union laws. Badly smashed during the colonial response to Positive Action in 1950, the trade unions were weak and dispersed. So long as the Trades Disputes Act stayed in force, they could be nothing else. But to repeal the Act, I was assured, would be 'premature'.

Thus a prime need for the new government was to gain parliamentary control of the civil service. Yet all through the six years of 'preparation' for independence, from 1951 to 1957, the C.P.P. found itself unable to do this. The colonial heritage stopped them at every turn.

There seems no doubt that Nkrumah pressed from the very first for democratic control of the machinery of government, and indeed the need for it was obvious. As things stood, the civil service was responsible neither to government nor parliament. C.P.P. ministers could urge new policies, and give orders to their permanent secretaries. But what they could not do, neither in 1951 nor in 1955 nor even under the independence constitution of 1957, was to appoint, dismiss, or even transfer the very men upon whom they had to rely for day-to-day administration. Whenever it came to a showdown, it was the Public Service Commission and the Governor who carried the day. Precious years were lost, and the building of a new democracy was dangerously delayed.

Consider, again, what happened in 1956 when a constitution for full political independence came at last under discussion. Nkrumah and his colleagues drew up draft proposals which would ensure a democratic control of the civil service. They called in the skilled and reliable help of a British advocate, Mr Geoffrey Bing, Q.C., who has since told the story in his important book, *Reap the Whirlwind*. In this crucial matter of controlling the civil service, they proposed that 'all executive powers relating to public officers and the public service generally shall be vested in the Governor-General', as the Governor was to become after independence, 'acting on the advice of the

Cabinet'. Government and ultimately parliament would thus obtain the right to appoint, dismiss or transfer its employees.

But London would not have it, even in 1956 with independence round the corner. Many of the senior civil servants were still British: were they now to become subject to African control? Not a bit of it. In Whitehall they examined the words I have just quoted, and revised them so as to keep things as they were. 'The appointment, promotion, transfer, termination of appointment, dismissal and disciplinary control of public officers,' they laid down, 'is hereby vested in the Governor-General acting on the advice of the Public Service Commission.' Only after 1960, when a republican constitution had abolished the office of Governor-General, and destroyed the duality of control under which the country had been ruled, was it possible for the government of Ghana to obtain full control of the civil servants whose salaries it paid.

In this, and in other such arrangements, lay the first great obstacle to the building of a nation: the colonial legacy of authoritarian rule and all the authoritarian attitudes fostered during the decades of foreign domination. This was the central weight of the colonial mountain, the hardest part to shove aside. And this was part of the burden, along with others, that 'prepared the way', not for independence, but for bitterness and strife.

A BLESSING AND A CURSE

After they had overthrown him, in 1966, the 'men of substance' and their friends abroad would say that Nkrumah had been handed a prosperous country and had ruined it, throwing away its national savings and plunging it into hopeless debt to foreign nations. Many foreigners rushed in to say this kind of thing, and worse. He was 'a master as hungry for wealth as he was for power', one of these asserted, a dictator whose 'monstrous robberies' had victimized a proud people confident of their future. Such things were also said by Ghanaians, including those who then proceeded to plunge the country still more deeply into debt, and to halve the value of its currency.

In Africa's later 'period of the warlords', there seemed nothing too bad to be said about the man who had constantly preached unity and peace. The triumph of political independence often came to seem a sham and a delusion. Even those Ghanaians who took power after Nkrumah, and set about expelling thousands of Nigerians and other foreign Africans from Ghana, accused him of racism. Even those Englishmen who afterwards had to deal with the expulsion of 30,000 Asians from Uganda joined eagerly in denigrating a man who had expelled nobody, except proven crooks or financial gangsters, and, however regrettably, two hostile journalists.

In 1951 there were as yet no accusations of personal greed against him, nor for several years after that. Nor was it then said that he was ruining the country. Foreign interests, if not Ghana's opposition, said that he was pursuing policies of sound expansion and development.

But this, too, was not true. Nkrumah's policies in the economic field were perfectly 'orthodox and respectable' during the six-year interval between 1951 and independence, and for a number of years after that. Yet they were sound neither in expansion nor in development. They were little more than a meek and often muddled acceptance of the economic dispositions of the colonial system. They followed the advice of foreign consultants who, however well-intentioned, wished above all to keep Nkrumah and his government loyal to the general economic structure of the capitalist world.

Nkrumah knew all this very well, even when least able to do anything about it. But he was not an economist; nor were any of his leading colleagues. Many of their major mistakes were made in the field of economic policy. And not a few of these flowed from misjudgements as to the wisdom, as distinct from the sincerity, of the foreign advisers who were employed. All this, too, he came to recognize in the last years, though a habit of loyalty to old friends seldom allowed him to say so.

Coming home in 1947, he had been aware of the general nature of the colonial system. Then and afterwards, he believed that the colonial system had worked to make the imperialist countries richer and the colonized countries poorer. This was one great reason why he considered that the key to progress lay in the seizure of political power. Only with that, he argued, could anything serious be done about the seizure of economic power. Win the political kingdom, he said, and the rest would be added.

The rest, as we know, has not been added. The Ghana of today has little more power over its economic destiny, over the ability to escape from inherited economic dependence, than the Gold Coast of 1951. How far was the fault Nkrumah's?

He started with small knowledge of the country's economic position, and even smaller means of changing it. Even after assuming office in 1951, when at least some of the necessary administrative files became available, his knowledge remained full of holes. In this, again, he was the captive of his circumstances. Nobody else knew much more. Even in the critical field of cocoa production, as the British economist Polly Hill has shown in her path-finding studies, the British had only a vague idea about the way that cocoa was produced and sold within the country. After all, they had no use for such knowledge. All they needed to be sure of was that cocoa could be purchased by the big trading companies on the coast. Who did the work among the Africans, or how they were paid amongst themselves, was useless knowledge.

Gradually, as one can see in his numerous writings, Nkrumah worked through to a detailed understanding of the system of production and exchange taken over by the C.P.P. from British colonial rule. He came to the conclusion that it remained a colonial system, even with Africans in charge of it. But little of this was clear during those early years of trying to win the political kingdom. Then it was a matter of riding the ill-assorted horses of political change and tactful negotiation: of moving from one month to the next, and solving daily problems as they came or setting them aside for solving later. But if Nkrumah tended for a long time to underestimate the true size of this part of the price for taking office, he had more excuse than lack of knowledge.

Ghana's main source of income, then as now, came from the export of cocoa. And the world price of cocoa was steadily on the rise. In 1949–50 the country had received £178 for each ton of cocoa sold abroad. In 1950–51 the figure rose to £269. In the two following years it was slightly lower. But in 1953–54 it reached £358 a ton, the highest figure ever paid till then. With cocoa as the country's economic mainspring, prosperity seemed assured. All that appeared necessary was to spend the money on modernization. Then as later, the truth was otherwise.

Why, for example, did the level of real wages, of wages in terms of what money will buy, stand *lower* at the end of Nkrumah's period of leadership than at the beginning of it? Why was the real income of Ghana's cocoa farmers, by far the biggest economic grouping in the country, generally no better in 1966 than in 1951? What explains this failure to improve the general standard of living of all those urban workers and farmers whose support had made political progress possible, and in whose name Nkrumah and the C.P.P. took office and then power?

*

The history of colonies shows that most of them have had a 'time of boom' at one period or another. Sometimes this boom came late in the colonial period, as during the 1950s in the Ivory Coast or the 1960s in Angola; sometimes it came early, as in Senegal and the Gold Coast. Early or late, the boom has derived from some new crop or product for export to the rest of the world. The French have found the most honest name for such booms. They have called them the *mises en valeur* of colonies, or, in plain English, 'the realizing of the profits'. History also shows that such 'expansion' has seldom continued for many years. But it lasts for long enough to 'freeze' the colony's way of life and labour into a pattern which does continue.

This is what happened with cocoa in Ghana when it was the Gold Coast. The country's farmers began producing this valuable crop in about 1890. Just a few tons then, but these sold well. Soon the demand began to soar. Around 1900 the country's farmers were selling some 2,000 tons a year, and by 1910 they were selling 40,000 tons. Making nonsense of all such talk as that Africans do not understand how to 'increase productivity', they became the world's greatest producers of cocoa.

What the independent government was able to do, thanks partly to relieving rural debt and other encouragements, was to make this cocoa boom continue. In 1960 Ghana achieved the enormous total of 350,000 tons. And in 1965, at the very time when Nkrumah's leadership was being said to have ruined the economy, they produced and sold no fewer than 494,000 tons, breaking all previous records. Yet through all this long-continued boom, the underlying economic system stayed the same. As we shall see, it was the economic consequences flowing from this system, underlying everything else, that were to lie at the basis of Nkrumah's final downfall.

So it was obviously the economic system, not the actual scale of production, which must have been responsible for continuing low cocoa incomes and urban wage levels. In the first place, then, to whom were Ghanaians selling all this cocoa? Not to other Ghanaians, for Ghanaians have little use for chocolate or other derivatives of the cocoa tree. From the first they were selling it to European firms; and these firms, banded together in their own interests, were able to fix the price they were willing to pay. Nkrumah understood this in a general way when he took office. Later he defined it more clearly. The enduring pattern of this 'monopolistic control', he wrote in 1963, 'was firmly set in the first quarter of the present century, when the pioneering firms and our own African "merchant princes", as they were called, were either forced out of business or absorbed by the giant companies'.

Now the objective of these companies was to make a large profit on their dealings; this, as they understandably explained, was their duty to shareholders in Europe. Consequently they bought as cheaply as they could. Steadily, over the years, the country's farmers were toiling at a crop which transferred wealth out of the country by transferring profits to London and other centres of the industrialized world.

The battle for the farmers, accordingly, was on two fronts. They had to wage war against the pests and diseases which threatened their crops. And they had to wrestle, as best they could, with the cocoa buyers. They needed these buyers, just as the buyers needed them; what they fought for was a better deal. They found it hard to get this; mostly they failed. Once the system was established, they became cogs in a great machine of supply beyond their means of control, or even, for the most part, of serious influence.

So it came about that the harder they worked and the more they produced, the lower the 'world price' tended to fall. In 1965, the year of their greatest crop, this price fell to the lowest point in modern times. The more they 'developed' the cocoa industry, in other words, the less money they received for their product. This was one main reason why the policies of development then in fashion, policies of making the *existing* economic system produce more, could not bring a higher standard of living. In any overall sense, applying to the nation as a whole, they were not policies of change but of no-change, not policies of development but merely of growth. And, as the cocoa industry showed so clearly, no such growth could guarantee a genuine and overall development. What it really guaranteed was another instalment of 'under-development', together with all the added political strains that go along with that.

In 1951 and after, the policies imposed on the C.P.P. government by the British, or accepted by the C.P.P. on the advice of their advisers, were all designed to maintain the existing economic system, and make it grow. Falling cocoa prices in years of high production were explained by the iron laws of 'supply and demand'. That was how the world was organized, there was nothing, really, you could do about it. All the same, it appeared that something should at least seem to be done about it; and the British, even before 1951, had hit upon an idea. As a Second World War imperialist arrangement, they had invented the Cocoa Marketing Board.

The idea was that in high-price years farmers would be paid less than the 'world price' of cocoa; and the difference would be placed in a reserve fund. In low-price years, on the other hand, farmers would be compensated from this fund. Things would thus be 'equalled out', and suffering averted. So it was arranged that all the cocoa should be sold to an official Board, and the Board would sell it to the European companies.

It sounded a good idea. If nothing could be done about the laws of supply and demand, at least this arrangement might balance the see-saw of cocoa incomes. But it turned out differently, as such things tend to do in colonial systems. What happened was that the Board made a handsome profit every year, and this profit was transferred to London. There it became part of Britain's general banking assets in the world at large. The money was not, of course, stolen; it remained the property of the Gold Coast Colony and Protectorate. But the Gold Coast did not use the money.

Hard up in the wake of all the sacrifices of the second world war, Britain needed all the sterling assets she could thus 'borrow' from her colonies. The cocoa reserve was accordingly kept in London. It might have been invested in making the Gold Coast Colony a better place to live in. In theory it could be so invested, but in practice it was not. On their side, the Gold Coast colonial government, and then the C.P.P. government after 1951, were in any case allowed to use only a small part of these forced savings so as to buy 'hard currency'. In 1953, the country earned about £25 millions from exports to the United States and other 'dollar area' countries; Nkrumah's government was allowed to use 21 per cent of these earnings. In 1954, such earnings were down to £20 millions; the part that Nkrumah's government was allowed to use fell to 16 per cent.

This was tough on development. But it was even tougher on the cocoa farmers. In 1953, to continue the same example, the Board sold cocoa to a total value of £74 millions. But the amount paid to cocoa producers was only £28 millions.

*

Now it was obvious to Nkrumah, pondering these curious arrangements, that Ghana was in fact helping to finance Britain's banking system. Somewhat lost in the complexities, and these were very complex, he decided that the right thing would be to employ some good foreign economists who could discover whatever might be done to change this. One of the men he wanted to engage was Dr (now Lord) Thomas Balogh, whom Britain's Labour prime minister was to employ as an economic adviser after 1964. But the Colonial Office in London did not approve; it would itself, if necessary, provide whatever advice might be required.

The advice that came was not very helpful. Most of it, in its general effect, was that the C.P.P. government should do nothing to rock the great imperial boat. Report after report insisted that the C.P.P. government must 'meet its commitments and so inspire the confidence without which foreign assistance, whether in the form of private investment, managerial ability, or financial assistance, will not be forthcoming'.* If the country insisted on spending its own money, it could expect to be penalized for foul play. Any thought that the country might be far better off if it spent its own money, and did without 'financial assistance', was regarded as silly and probably subversive.

Nkrumah was not fooled, but he had to bide his time. When independence came, the total of Ghana's holdings in London's sterling reserves totalled about £170 millions. It was not long before he had secured full control of them, and not long again

* Gold Coast, *Economic Survey*, 1954, para. 43.

before his independent government began to spend this money on modernization.

From this point of view one can say that the operations of the Cocoa Marketing Board eventually proved a blessing. They launched the country into political independence with a useful sum of money in its national pocket. Much of this money was usefully spent on roads and harbours, dams and schools and universities. Even in 1963 the country's capital reserves still stood at £73 millions, though by this time Nkrumah's critics were loud in their complaints of 'waste and ruin'. Would they have perhaps preferred that the money should have stayed in London's banking system?

From a larger point of view, the whole great cocoa enterprise proved a curse, and for two reasons. The first was that Ghana remained locked within an economic pattern of relying on exports of cocoa. The 'single crop economy' became a kind of prison. Many bad effects flowed from it. A concentration on producing food for export distracted farmers from the immediately less attractive task of growing food for Ghana's people. Food imports tended every year to rise. This meant spending abroad money which could have been spent more productively at home.

There was little effort in these circumstances to diversify production with the aim of manufacturing goods which Ghana must otherwise buy abroad. The colonial pattern was prolonged. Producing cocoa during the colonial period had 'made the economy grow'; it had done almost nothing to develop that economy into new forms and techniques of production. What it had helped to develop, on the contrary, was the economy of oversea countries to which the profits flowed.

Locked into this pattern, Ghana found it impossible to get out. Nkrumah and his governments tried hard, but they did not succeed. That is why Nkrumah began calling so urgently, after 1960, for the working unity of African countries: only such a unity, he urged, could give these ex-colonies the strength to break a system which, otherwise, would break them.

But there was a second and more immediate reason why the cocoa enterprise proved a curse. The Marketing Board had been partly launched as a means of compensating farmers for low incomes when the 'world price' of cocoa fell. Little by little, however, the reserves accumulated by the Marketing Board came to be regarded as national savings. Conservative C.P.P. ministers such as Komlo Gbedemah, in tune with their orthodox advisers, began to think that it would be wrong to distribute these savings to those who had earned them. And Nkrumah supported them in thinking this.

Yet these were still the savings of cocoa farmers. And cocoa farmers, reacting against their own incomes, felt increasingly that they were being robbed of an unreasonably large part of the fruits of their toil. All through the years when the C.P.P. was in office, but not yet in power, this feeling of resentment grew. Only a government of genuine mass participation could have assuaged it. But the compromise of 1951 made it ever harder for the C.P.P. government to act as a government of mass participation.

*

Working through the files, the C.P.P. ministers found much to surprise them. There was the remarkable case of the country's gold mines.

Already a gold exporter for some five hundred years from alluvial deposits and shallow mines, during the colonial period Ghana began to yield gold from deep mines bored by foreign companies. This was another aspect of the colonial 'realizing of the profits'. About this, too, Nkrumah and others knew something in theory. But they knew little in practice; too many facts had been hidden in the files. And they could learn few details from fellow-Africans: in 1951, for example, there was only one African geologist employed in the gold-fields, and no senior African accountant. Now the files taught them better.

Among documents available to them was a memorandum of 1951, written by a forthright British official and produced by the official printing office, but marked on the cover *Confidential* and *Limited Circulation*.* This pointed out that the whole mining industry was owned by foreign companies, employed many Europeans, and sent large funds abroad every year. Although the author had access to all official information, since he was Permanent Secretary of the Ministry of Commerce, Industry and Mines, he still found it impossible to make exact estimates of just how large these transferred funds really were. But he had a go at it, and, in doing so, produced a document of key importance to an understanding of the colonial system, whether in Ghana or anywhere else.

He took the year 1949, fairly typical of colonial years, and found that the gold-mining industry had then earned £6·4 millions. Of this total, he concluded, 'perhaps three million pounds can be considered to have been transferred abroad'. Diamonds in the same year had earned £1·4 millions: 'some £550,000 was transferred abroad'. Still in 1949, 'corresponding estimates for manganese place the funds remitted [abroad] at some £2 million out of an export total of £4 million [in earnings]'. All in all, it was 'a fair estimate' to say that the whole Ghana mining industry sent out to Europe and the U.S.A., colonial year by year, about *half* of its total earnings.

Could there be a more convincing proof that the development of the colonial economy was not the same, and could not be the same, as the development of the country as a whole? Wasn't it obvious that the growth of the mining industry helped Britain and the U.S.A., or other oversea investors, far more than it could possibly help Ghana? *Half* its earnings every year were going oversea; in other words, practically all its profits as well as a large part of the money-savings of its well-paid European technicians and executives. Only the crumbs remained at home where the ores were mined. Reading this kind of document, Nkrumah saw his early ideas about the colonial system resoundingly confirmed.

But it was just as obvious that there could be no chance of

* *Memorandum on Mining in the Gold Coast*, Accra, 1951.

applying these ideas before the coming of independence. The imperial attitude was that political concessions to the Africans should not endanger the existing economic situation. As his official advisers were busy recommending, the C.P.P. government must ensure confidence abroad by 'meeting its commitments': that is, by agreeing to stay inside the colonial economic pattern. Nothing else, they said as though it were a truth that could not be denied, was properly thinkable.

The same memorandum said it too. This vast transfer of earnings abroad, with the subsequent conversion of these earnings into investment capital in the 'developed' countries instead of in Ghana, was 'necessarily involved in the operation of the mining industry as a whole'. *Necessarily*, please note: either no mining in Ghana, or mining with the profits sent abroad. Not only that: 'this tendency for earnings to leave the country is likely to be reinforced by the expansion of the industry'.

And why should such earnings 'tend' to leave the country? Because they didn't like the tropics, felt uneasy in African hands, preferred to rest in the safe deposits of banks in London? Not exactly. It was because their owners were in London, and, explained the memorandum, 'it is fair to assume that expansion will only take place if the mining operators can see their way to increasing their profits, and if some political stability is guaranteed'.

The sting was in the tail. 'Political stability' meant economic stability; and economic stability, in plain language, meant 'no change'. Anything else would be reckless or impossible: in a thousand different voices, some friendly and others not, the same lesson was chanted in those months and years by officials, specialists and advisers of every stripe.

For the time being, Nkrumah knew that he would have to accept this lesson, knowing too that it was false. Not far from his office, in private houses such as that of Dr Danquah, the 'men of substance' warned that C.P.P. threats to tax these transferred earnings would frighten off the bringers of foreign capital. To Nkrumah, at least, it was obvious that these 'men of substance' had a very poor grasp of what they were talking about. No foreign investor able to reap and remove profits on the existing scale was going to be frightened off by its mere reduction.

The big question, the only real question, was a different one. How to escape from the inherited colonial pattern? How to add economic gains to political gains? This was the question that was going to probe and worry at him for the rest of his life. Meanwhile, somehow or other, he had to make the compromise with Governor Arden-Clarke work well enough to yield an independence in which 'stability' need no longer mean 'no change'. In this, again, he stood head and shoulders above the men of the opposition. They saw no further than their noses, and not always very well as far as that. But his own eyes were on these big questions of the future.

He was obliged to begin by swallowing much that he had formerly rejected; and above all by setting aside all his convictions about the need for economic change. This was the only way, so far as he could see, to make the compromise yield the substance as well as the shadow of independence. So it was that much was done that later would be bitterly regretted.

He embarked on what he called 'tactical action'. To some of of his old friends, it looked very like a sell-out. Far better, they thought, to refuse office even now, and to fight for an entirely fresh start. Such ideas seemed mere 'big talk' to Nkrumah, even if he sympathized with the thought behind them. Others among his colleagues, notably Komlo Gbedemah, did not sympathize in the least with that thought; they held that such ideas were foolish or perverse. Only a handful continued to believe in rejecting the compromise.

Here again one needs to recall the atmosphere of that period. The British during the early 1950s might be prepared to make political concessions in the Gold Coast, provided always that these concessions did not threaten the economic pattern. But in nearly all other parts of black Africa the colonial system seemed to be growing stronger and more aggressive. Only in

Nigeria were there real signs of political progress, and even these were doubtful ones until Nkrumah set the pace in 1951. Kenya was plunged then into the prelude to an emergency in which the British Army would try to smash the nationalist cause on behalf of a small white farming community of settlers and their business interests, and some 10,000 Kenya Africans would lose their lives.

Further south, in Southern Rhodesia, other white settlers were about to win control not only of their own colony, for this they had already, but also of Northern Rhodesia (Zambia) and Nyasaland (Malawi). They eventually failed; but no one could be sure of this at the time, for the odds were stacked high on the settler side. Nearly all the French colonies were in the grip of administrative repression, their leaders tracked by the police or stopped in their work. A grim silence brooded over the vast colonies of Portugal.

Nkrumah's problem was to make the compromise yield progress for Ghana's sake, but also, as he saw it, for Africa's as well. And these were indeed the years when Ghana and the C.P.P. became a beacon of hope for embattled nationalists across the continent, looking to Nkrumah and the C.P.P., as they undoubtedly did, as pioneering heroes who would broaden the breach they had made, and give others the chance of following through it. Anyone who travelled much in black Africa in those days knows that this was true. Even in the heart of the huge and voiceless Belgian Congo, even in the solitudes of Angola and Mozambique, there would come the whispered questions: 'Is it really like that? Do they have an African government up there?'

Everything that Nkrumah had ever believed about the cause of African freedom and unity combined now to convince him that almost any compromise would be worthwhile, provided only that he could still make it yield a real political progress. As it was, the pressures brought to bear upon the C.P.P. government forced Nkrumah and his ministers to act within narrow limits. These pressures were British and colonial. But they were also African and traditional.

TRIBES OR A NATION?

Back in the past, before the 1870s, most of Ghana had been united within the Ashanti empire. Destroying that empire, British imperial power had destroyed its unity. Under colonial rule, the country went back to its still earlier condition of a multitude of small states. These states were not of course independent in colonial times. But they represented internal political divisions with a strong life of their own. They were the first barricades on the African side through which Nkrumah had to lead the C.P.P.

Far in the north, beyond the forests of Ashanti, there were the 'Northern Territories', inhabited by peoples who belonged, for the most part, to the languages, customs and beliefs of the Western and Central Sudan. They had chiefs of their own through whom the British also ruled; or else they were small and close-knit societies that barely looked beyond the limits of their village lives. Either way, the messengers of national unity found it hard to make themselves heard. It was a long time before the C.P.P. would win a good position there.

Ashanti in its hills and forests was the core of the old pre-colonial empire. Here lay much of the country's exportable wealth, whether of minerals, cocoa, or timber. Most of the people who produced this wealth were ruled by chiefs whose power derived from distant ancestors and venerable habits of popular obedience. Presiding over this hierarchy of chiefs was the Asantehene, the king who stood in the line of the old emperors. He was the richest of all the Ashanti nobles. So long as he and his fellow-nobles observed the orders or the wishes of the British commissioner in the Ashanti capital of Kumasi, an official whose own position was not unlike that of a king, they were sure to keep their privileges and positions. Nationalism, for them, came as a personal threat far more than a promise of progress.

Not surprisingly, most of them and their dependants were furiously opposed to the C.P.P. They soon looked at Nkrumah as a grimy demon who had climbed up from the nether regions so as to imperil their wealth and comfort. They criticized the British from time to time, and even made occasional speeches about freedom and independence. But they never forgot, when it came to the point of action, that colonial rule had buttressed their own importance. For the great effect of colonial rule was to divide its subjects, and play them off against each other. This is one large reason why 'tribalism' was to plague the newly-independent states. Each network of chiefs and local dignitaries, recognized by colonial rule and given privileges, tended to try and keep its position over against the others.

South of Ashanti, towards the coast, there were peoples whose chiefs had sided with the British, long before, so as to throw off the overlordship of the Ashanti empire. This was where the early colony had taken shape by an agreement between these chiefs and the British of the nineteenth century. But this was also the area where the new ideas of nationalism and independence had taken hold. Yet even this southern area—the 'Colony proper' as distinct from the 'Protectorate' of Ashanti and the 'Northern Territories'—was far from being a unity. When Nkrumah took office there were no fewer than sixty-six different 'states' in the Colony alone. Each had made its own 'treaty' with the colonial power. Each retained its own local loyalties. These were weaker than local loyalties in Ashanti and the North. But they still counted for a lot.

And when Nkrumah took office the whole great pomp and panoply of imperial patronage was still in full display. Dazzling and brilliant ceremonies, such as only the peoples of West Africa know how to mount and celebrate, were devoted to the honours of the King-Emperor in London; or, as it now fell out, to the Queen-Emperor. I remember attending one of these when the Konor Mate Kole of Manya Krobo was awarded an imperial honour within a few months of the C.P.P.'s taking office. While vast umbrellas twirled and shook their many-coloured fringes, their domes swaying in the sun, the Konor came forth in splendid costume, robed in the manner of his ancestors, immensely dignified, to receive the gifts of imperial recognition.

This was royal history repeated in all the splendour of tradition. Drums beat their messages of greeting and announcement. Dignitaries on either hand went through the nobles' minuets of majesty. For his part, as I recall, the Konor made an interesting speech. He told how his grandfather had received an admiral's uniform from the government of Denmark; how Queen Victoria, greatest monarch of imperial Europe, had honoured his father with a medal and appointed him to be Knight of the Victorian Order; and now of his own emotion at receiving the Order of the British Empire. It was an old imperial custom; and the Konor was gently proud of it.

The Konor, as it happened, was a man who looked at the future as well as at the past. Many of the great nobles found that unwise or disagreeable. Most of them turned their backs, as rudely as they could, upon the messengers of nationalism. Even in 1957 the king of Ashanti found himself 'too busy' even to attend the independence celebrations in his country's capital. In earlier years his hostility was complete.

'You people are traitors, quislings and fifth columnists,' one of the great Ashanti chiefs had told the young nationalists of Ashanti back in 1948: those, such as Krobo Edusei, who had worked and spoken for the nationalist cause even before the C.P.P. was born. Hauling Krobo and others before him, the Asantehene had lashed out at them. 'During the recent unrest in Ashanti, we maintained silence, and watched you with a philanthropic contempt. We were convinced, and we were not wrong, that you would reach nowhere.' It was still to be a long time, more than ten years, before these powerful nobles understood that it was they, and not the youngmen, who had 'reached nowhere'. All these attitudes were part of the burden that the C.P.P. was bound to assume. They help to explain the ways in which the C.P.P. assumed it.

These old loyalties were made powerful by history and religion. The nationalists had to find ways of demonstrating that their own loyalties were also supported by history and religion. Against the power of the divine ancestors, they now opposed the belief that nationalism was the rightful future that should grow from the loyalties of the past. Soon enough, they began to build a cult of Nkrumah on ancestral lines. But when they chanted 'Nkrumah Never Die', it was not because they thought the man immortal, any more than the Asantehene and other great chiefs were immortal. At least at the beginning, it was because they wished to claim for Nkrumah a spiritual power as great as that of the chiefs. And when they gave Nkrumah the old title of *Osagyefo*, it was because they wished to oppose that to other such titles, not least to that of the Asantehene, *Otumfuo* or 'All-Powerful'.

The cult got seriously and dangerously out of hand, and gradually helped to undermine Nkrumah's own grasp of reality. But in those days the battle for national unity was also a battle against the disunity of the past and present, and against all the beliefs upon which that disunity had come to rest. The youngmen did not always fight it wisely, but they fought it as they could.

There were other disunities hard to deal with. Like many colonial frontiers, Ghana's divided several peoples. Of these the most important were the Ewe (Ev-vay) in the south-east of the country. Some Ewe were within the frontiers of neighbouring Togo. Others were within the frontiers of the Gold Coast Colony. When the nationalist cause was on the rise, the Ewe of the Gold Coast were in disagreement about what they should do. Some wished to stay inside the Ghana nation of the C.P.P. Others clamoured for unification with their fellow-Ewe in Togo, then a French colony: for them, the Ewe nation was more important than the Ghana nation. It came about that Governor Arden-Clarke's last official act, before handing over power in 1957, was to send troops into Trans-Volta so as to repress an Ewe revolt against the new government.

Nkrumah's own belief about this kind of problem, formed in the distant days of Pan-African debate at Lincoln and Philadelphia, was that the interests which united neighbouring

African peoples must always be greater than other interests which divided them. His own Nzima people were also divided between two colonies, Gold Coast and Ivory Coast. They might stay divided for local administrative purposes; but their true interests could be realized, he thought, only within an overall unity on federal lines.

Back again at home, he was forced to play the game the way the cards were stacked, because there was no other way to play it. And the way the cards were stacked was strongly in favour of local interests, and strongly against any federal plan. All the aces and 'court cards' in the pack were on the side of the dividers of Africa. Some of these cards were held by local chiefs and business interests; others were held by the colonial powers. Both played these cards for all they were worth.

The local dividers played them in defence of their own particular local interests. The colonial powers played them in defence of their political and economic 'spheres of interest'. They had no intention of abandoning these. To the very last the imperial powers insisted on the absolute 'integrity' of their 'spheres', and contacts between neighbouring nationalist movements were cut to a minimum, especially by the French.

French West Africa had been divided into eight territories (with Togo, a Trusteeship Territory taken over in 1918 from its German colonizers, forming a ninth). All these were ruled from Dakar as a colonial federation. That is why the greatest of the nationalist parties in French West Africa, the Rassemblement Démocratique Africain (R.D.A.), was able to begin as a federal party: a single party with 'sections' in each of the territories. Some of its wisest leaders hoped to transform the colonial federation into an independent one, and so, from the start, unite a vast area of West Africa.

But French governments had no mind for any such thing. A large federal state such as this would be might be able to defend itself; they preferred to break up their colonial federation and make sure that a weak political independence came separately to each of its territories. That is what they did in

1956, when each territory was accorded the same kind of 'internal self rule' as the C.P.P. had won for Ghana five years earlier. In this way decolonization became a new kind of 'balkanization', a further breaking up of Africa into separate states which, being poor and small in population, were also weak states.

Nkrumah marked this process well, and lost no chance of saying so. Not many were ready to listen to him then. In this, as in much else, he was ahead of his time. If that was to prove his tragedy, it was also to provide a measure of the man's far-ranging insight. But the first task, in any case, was to build a unity within Ghana. It was bound to be a gruelling test. How far would the C.P.P. be capable of meeting it?

A PARTY OF THE POOR, OR A PARTY OF THE PRIVILEGED?

'Red Shadow over the Gold Coast', shrieked Britain's chief Conservative newspaper, the *Daily Telegraph*, on 17 October 1950; and the cry of 'communism' would become a refrain through all the years that followed. It dwindled in volume whenever Nkrumah and the C.P.P. stayed obediently in line with 'Western interests'. It rose again to an uproar whenever they did not.

In fact, what kind of party was the C.P.P.?

A movement of the poor and humble, of what George Padmore called 'the plebeian masses': that is how Nkrumah saw the ranks of nationalism when he came home and led them. For a while, that is how it really was.

Early in 1951, when Nkrumah and the other 'prison graduates' were still inside James Fort, an English observer paid a visit to the outside of it. Its 'only claim to fame', he wrote in *West Africa*, was 'that it housed the man whose name was on every lip—Kwame Nkrumah. Outside the gates three well-dressed women have alighted from a highly polished limousine. They are relatives of the C.P.P. prisoners.'

Across the road, watching, this observer then notices a boy in tattered shorts leaning on a battered bicycle. What does this boy of the people think about the scene? 'He points beyond the limousine and shouts. What is his message? Abuse of rich Africans? Or of the European prison officials? But listen to what he says: "There is victory for us, in the struggle of the C.P.P." . . .'*

In those tumultuous days the power of the C.P.P. lay with the people in the streets and the villages: if this was 'communism', then the *Daily Telegraph* was right. The men of substance might claim to speak for African opinion. But it was not to the members of the Accra Turf Club and the Gold Coast Bar Association that the people in the streets and villages looked for leadership, nor to their kind of language that they listened. Their heroes were the youngmen of the elementary schools whose gifts were for strong talk and vivid action, the scribes of little newspapers that spoke in words of dramatic force and urgency; and it was Nkrumah who embodied all these.

It was the youngmen who bore the heat and burden of the struggle. They carried the message of 'self-government NOW' to every part of the coastal areas, travelling in hopeless old cars whenever they could, walking or begging lifts whenever they must. They carried it into the villages of Ashanti; they made Kumasi ring with their demands. They even carried it into the silent plains of the North.

All this they did on a shoe-string. Self-sacrifice was the order of the day. In later years Nkrumah recalled how he had urged members to follow the advice of the Chinese:

> 'Go to the people,
> Live among them
> Love them
> Serve them . . .'

And the party activists did so to the utmost of their capacity and understanding. The C.P.P. could never otherwise have

* Issue of 17 February 1951.

triumphed, for in those days the C.P.P. had everything against it save popular support.

It was not a *party* in any close-knit sense, least of all the kind of organized, disciplined and intellectually prepared party such as could have propagated 'communism' or any other complex doctrine. Like every nationalist movement of those days, the C.P.P. had no detailed doctrine of thought and action. Ideology was precisely what it did not have, unless ideology is a mere longing to be free. There had been no time for deep thought about the future, or for any general understanding of the need for such thought. The C.P.P. was swept along on a tide of impatience to be finished with foreign rule.

Yet the C.P.P. was also something else than an upsurge of the poor and humble. It was more than that, and also different from that. It gathered the spokesmen of urban workers and country farmers in its ranks. But it gathered others too, and these others soon acquired the leadership. Who were they? It is hard to give them a label. 'Petty bourgeois' is perhaps the nearest English term for their social condition, though far from an exact one.

These men and women who acquired the leadership were not among the people of substance who placed their bets at the Turf Club—at least in those days—or aired their views in the meetings of the Bar Association. Nor were they sure of anything but a rude reception in the palaces of kings and chiefs. Many were small clerks or traders: a sort of 'lower middle class' between the poor and humble on one side, and the men of substance on the other. Most had an eye on the material and financial advantages which might accrue to membership of a nationalist party which could succeed. They needed the poor and humble, but rather as the foot-sloggers of an army are needed by its officers.

There was nothing special about the C.P.P. in this respect. All the independence movements of those days were led by this kind of people. Colonial government would give way only to mass pressure. But mass pressure called for a leadership which

was at least sufficiently educated in European ways to be able
to formulate demands, and devise tactics, that colonial government would find effective. This became the role of the 'petty
bourgeoisie', of the 'lower middle class' in colonial Africa.

But it happened in Ghana's case, and perhaps this was rather
special, that the country's 'petty bourgeoisie' was numerous and
energetic. Its ranks were constantly enlarged by the sheer multi-
plicity of the country's trading enterprises. Thus the 'market
women' of Accra, among Nkrumah's most powerful supporters
in the capital, were not just a picturesque set of portly handsome ladies peddling wares in the street. They were key links
in the chain of distribution, handling goods to the value of
thousands of pounds every month. Great European trading
companies depended on them; these companies could not otherwise have organized the wholesale trade. Like many of the men
who rose to leadership in the C.P.P., business was in the life-
blood of these energetic women. Business was what they understood to their fingers' tips; and the interests of business were
the driving interests in their nationalism.

So it was that the triumph of the C.P.P. rested on a major
contradiction within itself. What gave the party its strength
was the support of masses of ordinary people in town and
village. In this respect the C.P.P. was a profoundly radical movement. But what gave the party its leadership was precisely this
'petty bourgeoisie', radical only in its language and soon not
even in that, for whom the gains of nationalism became increasingly a passport to privilege and personal enrichment.

This contradiction was always there, but not always obvious.
Often it was obscured by the 'plebeian' origin of many of the
new leaders: by the lack of definition 'at the edges' that was
always displayed by the social affiliations of this lower middle
class. Often it was blurred by the language and attitudes of
those days. Many of the petty bourgeois leaders believed
ardently in the cause of Africa's liberation, and suffered much
for the sake of it. Yet it soon appeared that they would tend,
as the early gains were won, to put their personal interests first;

and it was not long before the tendency became a habit. They were not averse to Nkrumah's talking fervently of unity and national freedom; so long as he merely talked, they enjoyed the fame and respect that all this brought to Ghana and themselves. But their eyes became ever more firmly fixed on interests and advantages which had little or nothing in common with unity and national freedom. It was all very understandable; and not in the least peculiar to Africa, much less to Ghana. But it was also very damaging to unity and national freedom.

Nkrumah's gift and virtue, and the reason why he could achieve so much in these conditions, was that he knew how to rise above this contradiction in his party, and to see the present always as the gateway to a different future. Yet rising above a contradiction of this kind is not the same as resolving it, and he did not resolve it. One may well think that no one, then, could have resolved it, and that the resolution of this inner conflict of aims and methods could lie only in the future, in years of struggle against economic colonization. However that may be, Nkrumah remained a man of his place and period, and the contradiction in his party remained a contradiction in himself as well. It led to much of his flamboyance, indulgence in display, uncertainty of personal judgement, and readiness to play the game the way that others played it.

Though himself nothing of a trader, he led a party which became, increasingly, a traders' party with a traders' attitude to politics. And the six-year compromise with colonial rule, with things-as-they-were between 1951 and 1957, was also a compromise with that particular trend and style, and steadily reinforced it. After 1960, when the hard days returned, Nkrumah said that the C.P.P. must again become a party of the masses. But by this time life itself had resolved the contradiction in another way, and the C.P.P. had become a party of the privileged. Then he was obliged to stand alone; and in that solitude he fell.

That is looking a long way ahead of the early and middle fifties. He was far from isolated then, and the degeneration of the C.P.P. was not yet upon the list of his worries. Flushed with success, the party saw him as the embodiment of all its hopes, and the party then, beyond any doubt, spoke for the poor and humble in a voice that was their own. The problem was not to transform the C.P.P., but to choose a line of action which could carry it to further success.

There was really no effective choice. If Nkrumah chose 'tactical action', it was because the compromise allowed no other way. And so it came about that these were the years of full retreat from radical ideas and modes of action. Could it have been different? Did Nkrumah go too far, much farther than he need have gone, in this 'tactical action' of compromise? It is easy to think that he did.

But it is hard to be sure. They were immensely difficult years, pioneering, testing, full of harsh obstructions. They hurried him along from one crisis to the next. No sooner had he overcome one of these than he had to face another. And they were also years of great success.

SWING TO THE RIGHT

Having accepted the compromise with Arden-Clarke, Nkrumah worked for its fruits with the 'tactical action' which, he joked a little defensively, might also be called 'tactful action'. He was tremendously tactful. He was moderate. He was flexible. He was willing to listen to the most orthodox advice.

The British were surprised: this was not at all the man they had imagined. The old opposition of the U.G.C.C., now in more or less total disarray, were enraged, and denounced Nkrumah for betraying the national cause by which, it was patently clear, they really meant their own cause.

Most of the new leaders of the C.P.P. were delighted: Nkrumah, they found, was after all a man of their own kind. But there were others in the C.P.P. leadership, the minority of the radical wing who had led the Positive Action campaign of 1949, who were not delighted. 'Tactical action', for them, had all the smell of defeat.

They were few; and few listened to them. Fewer still approved of what they said. Yet they had their weight in the councils of the party, and their discontent was among the first of Nkrumah's troubles. He tried to head off their complaints. But they had none of his belief that the compromise could be made to work in ways the British would not like.

As a 'critical group' within the executive of the party they were identified by Nkrumah's *Evening News* as early as December 1951. The majority on the executive, it was then explained, had reasoned tolerantly with them, and pointed out the error of their ways. But the reasoning was not enough. In April 1952 there came the first expulsions of half a dozen critics. A month later the executive expelled several more. These men retired into the wings, sure that the C.P.P. was on the wrong track.

Some of them counted for little on the political scene. Of such was Bankole Awooner-Renner, he who had remarked to me a few months earlier that the initiative had passed 'from the hands of the oppressed to the hands of the oppressors'. A large but frail figure who had suffered in prison, he was disgusted by the behaviour of those C.C.P. leaders of the 'traders' faction' who were already getting their hands into the honeypot, or were said to be doing so in gossip at the time. He thought that the British were simply giving the C.P.P. enough rope to hang itself. Later he abandoned his radical aims and joined forces with the conservative opposition, becoming leader of a splinter party called the Moslem Association.

But there were others who counted for more. Among these were the leaders of a trade union movement now struggling to recover from its wounds of 1950. Three of them had played a great part in that year and in 1949. These were Anthony Woode, Turkson Ocran, and Pobee Biney. All had gone to prison for their pains.

Emerging from prison, they set about forming an independent trade union organization in rivalry with the colonial-sponsored Gold Coast Trades Union Congress. This latter was a very tame affair. Translated from the motherland, the British colonial idea about trades unions was that they must never be 'political': their sole and manifest duty was to make the existing system work better, not to change it. Any effort to change it would be subversion; and subversion was a crime, probably promoted by Moscow.

Woode and his comrades did not see their duty in that light. They thought that an independent trades union organization could and should be an active arm in the struggle for far-reaching economic change; and this, of course, was nothing if not a highly political standpoint.

They denounced the political corruption that was already on the scene, though as yet of small importance. They derided the cult of Nkrumah's personality that sycophants were beginning to inflate. They made speeches about the need for higher wages. They went abroad and attended gatherings which, in those days of freezing Cold War between West and East, seemed a flagrant denial of the 'respectability' which 'tactical action' now preached. They began to be a serious annoyance to the 'respectable' inside the C.P.P. leadership. Intent on winning the political kingdom by tactical compromise, Nkrumah shared in this annoyance.

The fact was that the enthusiasm of 1951 had greatly ebbed. It was all too easy for the poor and humble to observe the C.P.P. leadership in its newly-found comfort, and to wonder if these leaders were going to do more than feather their own nests. That is what the old men of substance had always done: were these new men of substance any better? At least for these critics, the atmosphere of 1952 was one of let-down, and there was much to suggest that many of the voters found it so.

By the time of the party's third annual conference, in August 1952, such critics in the leadership had grown in number, being joined by a lawyer named Kurankyi Taylor and two journalists, Eric Heymann and Cecil Forde. They thought the compromise had gone too far, the pace of movement towards self-government too slow. They were still in a minority on the executive, and were told to accept the majority's decisions: otherwise, Nkrumah warned, there would be 'chaos and confusion'. Fresh expulsions were avoided for a while.

Nkrumah was meanwhile making his bow on the world scene, visiting America and other countries with an impressive and agreeable success. But early in 1953 he moved to regain the political initiative at home. After discussions in the party, on 10 July that year, he rose in the Assembly to move what he called his 'Motion of Destiny'. 'As soon as the necessary administrative arrangements are made', this ran, the British government 'should introduce an Act of Independence into the United Kingdom Parliament, declaring the Gold Coast a sovereign and independent state within the Commonwealth'. Meanwhile, 'as a matter of urgency', the British should agree to an all-African legislature; this should have full responsibility for all members of the Cabinet.

The wording was cautious but foreshadowed what would soon happen. To make sure it happened, 'respectability' remained the keynote. And the British, as though to reinforce the point, let fall at this time a strong warning of what they might still do, if there were any departure from 'respectability'. In October, far away across the Atlantic but very near in its possible parallel, London suddenly suspended the constitution of British Guiana because its independence party under Dr Cheddi Jagan was considered to be 'communist', notably by the government of the United States. Full colonial rule was reimposed on Guiana. Troops were sent to make it so.

If that could happen in Guiana, might it not in Ghana too? In Ghana, after all, the men of substance were rushing back and forth to London, issuing private and public appeals to the British that they should by no means give independence to the 'wild men' of the C.P.P., and above all not to any party led by Kwame Nkrumah. Several British newspapers were in full cry against the C.P.P. and its leader.

In a period when all radical voices were regularly denounced in British governing circles as 'reckless' or 'communist' or both, the warning from Guiana reached the C.P.P. leadership on top

E

of others of the same kind. It appeared that the C.P.P. could no longer afford its own radicals unless they were prepared to shut up. Besides which, most C.P.P. leaders had in any case a horror of anything that savoured of politically radical thought.

In October the executive majority moved accordingly against the radicals. They sacked Turkson Ocran from the C.P.P.-backed Trades Union Congress. They suspended Anthony Woode from the Party. They expelled Kurankyi Taylor. Nkrumah himself heralded a campaign against 'communist ideas'. One of the reasons given for suspending Woode was that he had attended a meeting, in Europe, of the East-backed World Federation of Trade Unions. Under Ocran's successor at the T.U.C., John Tettegah, the Ghana organization was duly inscribed, in 1954, as a member of the West-backed International Confederation of Free Trade Unions.

All this, in truth, had nothing to do with communism in Ghana, for there was no such thing, and almost nothing to do with 'communist ideas'. What Woode and his friends were really saying, it would seem, was that the C.P.P. must remain a party of strong popular participation; their real opposition was to the growing influence of the 'traders' faction'. No doubt Nkrumah knew this. But he failed to sympathize. What would have happened now if he had backed the radicals must remain one of the most tantalizing 'if's' of modern African history. With the British quite anxious by now to continue their controlled political withdrawal, could he not have mobilized the C.P.P. on a radical basis and still succeeded? As it was, he backed the 'traders' faction', and stuck to his programme of progress by tactful compromise. No one can be sure that he was wrong.

So it was that this move against the radicals, few though they were, came to have its major importance for the future. For in so moving, the C.P.P. shifted its base still further to the centre, and, so far as such European terms had a meaning in colonial Africa, also to the right. It spurred the leadership into strengthening the central organization of the party so as better o control the party's many branches in the country. In due course this strong accent on centralism was to have its bad effect. Instead of supervising the central command with active criticism, the branches were gradually reduced to a faceless chorus of assent.

Given the party's burgeoning numbers—perhaps 700,000 members by the middle of 1952, organized in some 500 branches—a more effective organization at headquarters in Accra was surely desirable. But the effect, with this swing to the right, was steadily to enlarge the power of the party bureaucracy at the expense of the popular voice and participation. This in turn tended to swell the number of 'beneficiaries' for whom the fight for self-government became increasingly the fight for personal advantage in job or salary, or access to lucrative trading contacts. The full damage to party democracy was to be seen only in the future, when the C.P.P. would decline into a self-perpetuating machine with little or no concern for its members 'at the base'. But that was not yet.

For the moment, 'tactical action' reaped its fruits in political advance. Expulsion of the radicals was duly noted by the British with approval, and taken as evidence that the C.P.P. leaders were going to 'act responsibly'. No doubt a radical government in London would have favoured a radical C.P.P.; as it was, Britain's Labour ministers had long been fearful of 'going too fast', which is just what their Conservative opponents, who were now in power, had vehemently said they were doing.

Another fruit of the compromise began to ripen. Rumours of political corruption became common talk. Nkrumah insisted on an official commission of inquiry. Chaired by a distinguished Ghanaian judge, it did not report until 1954. Then it found that allegations of general misconduct among C.P.P. ministers 'were not substantiated'. But it had some hard things to say about several of them. And one minister, a man of excellent repute, had already felt obliged to resign, admitting that as minister of communications and works he had received £2,000 from an Armenian contractor. The details revealed that the minister in question was guilty only of an indiscretion. But the whole affair fed the flames of gossip, and helped to widen once again the gap in confidence now widening between the voters and the leaders.

WORM IN THE FRUIT

How serious was corruption in those years? It is a subtle and complex subject, given all the circumstances whether of the distant or the recent past. It ranged across the whole social scene, and was very variously regarded. Colonial law, after all, was imposed law: if you could get round it, you might really be behaving rather well. Or else, of course, you might merely be behaving like a great many other people in other lands.

Scene in the ocean-port of Sekondi/Takoradi, shortly before the C.P.P. took office:

A bar late at night. Two or three tables and chairs under a bare electric bulb. At left, door to street. At right, bar-counter with glasses and bottles.

Two American seamen are drinking with a British seaman. The latter is in fact a British official concerned with suppression of drug-running, but the American seamen do not know this. He is paying for their drinks. They are drinking plenty.

One of the Americans pulls out a bag, dribbles marijuana from its corner.

'Where can I get rid of that?'

'What would you get,' asks the British seaman, 'if they caught you with that in the U.S.A.?'

'Twenty years, I guess.'

'Well, it's pretty hot here.'

'Thanks, buddy,' says the seaman, stowing away bag. Exit second seaman.

'Where's he gone?'

'Up to the cop shop,' confides the first American.

Enter second American with detective friend, an African. First seaman again brings out bag of hash. Detective suddenly recognizes British seaman, springs to attention. Tables overturned. Rapid getaway of two Americans . . .

This little scene was described for me by the British official in question. It happened in an ocean port that was notorious for its whores and drink shops. Pursuing a doctoral thesis in sociology, Dr Kofi Busia had lately completed a memorable inquiry into the condition of Sekondi/Takoradi. Prostitutes there could earn what was then a princely wage of £8 to £15 a month. They worked with 'pilot boys' who 'steered' the incoming seamen. These kids expected eight shillings in every pound of twenty shillings for their 'piloting', and could apparently earn from £3 to £6 a month.

A far cry from corruption in high places, no doubt, but this was also the general social ground and atmosphere in which the independence movements, somehow or other, had to stand firm and make progress. They had to work against a strong current of contempt or indifference for the laws and morals of colonial rule. They had to operate in times of great social dislocation, of rapidly growing towns, of profound moral disarray as old traditions of behaviour gave way to new conditions of daily life. They had to try for high standards of personal disinterestedness among followers who were much concerned, and even very understandably concerned, with immediate material gains.

If these movements had really been what the colonial powers sometimes feared they were, and what newspapers like the *Daily Telegraph* regularly said they were—highly-organized instruments of revolution—they might have fought clear of this many-sided heritage of past and present. They were anything but that. They opened their doors to all and sundry, if only because there was nothing else that they could do; and many among the all and sundry moved in for a personal kill.

Nkrumah had seen it coming. In 1951 he warned against the dangers that would follow upon taking office. Accepting a constitution 'which still makes us half-slave and half-free' would have great temptations, above all because C.P.P. leaders might 'be swayed by considerations of personal temporary advantage instead of seeking the interests of the people'.

'Hence we call for vigilance and moral courage, to withstand the evil manoeuvring of imperialism. Now bribery and corruption, both moral and factual, have eaten into the whole fabric of our society, and these must be stamped out if we are to achieve any progress.' They were not stamped out.

Nor, in the circumstances, could they be. This failure was not mainly because large numbers of people were relatively new to the temptations that come with the rise of a 'money economy'. It was not in any great degree because African tradition supposed that a man with a well-paid job would 'spread the benefits' widely among relatives, and would thus be always short of cash, no matter how much he might legitimately earn. It was certainly nothing special to the C.P.P., as corruption in subsequent Ghanaian regimes would duly prove; and it was just as certainly nothing special to Africa.

Above all, it was because the compromise supposed the growth of a middle class, of an entrepreneurial or bureaucratic bourgeoisie, who were expected to grow numerous and rich enough to dominate the political and economic life of the country. This was what all orthodoxy, all respectability, all 'sound behaviour' invariably supposed. And the historical fact remains that all such budding middle classes have just as invariably done their growing by a process of fraud and corruption. Britain's own budding middle class, back in the eighteenth century, had helped to lead the way.

Corruption in Nkrumah's time existed in high places and in low. Its overall economic damage, at least until the last years, was small. This damage was regularly exaggerated in foreign criticism which often appeared to revel in every indication of African dishonesty, rather as though scandals of corruption were unknown in Europe or America. But the political and moral damage was undoubtedly large, and confirmed the decline of the C.P.P.

Yet 1954, and even more 1955 and 1956, showed that Nkrumah's party was still, in spite of the swing to the right, a powerful magnet for mass loyalty and a strong vehicle for collective action. Given the problems now on the scene, it greatly needed to be both.

'FORWARD EVER . . .'

By the middle of 1953, when Nkrumah had again grasped the political initiative with his Motion of Destiny demanding full independence, the country was beginning to seethe once more with political excitement.

Now with two years' experience of office, he was in his element. The end of the compromise might at last be near. He worked harder than ever. Besieged by supplicants even in the middle of the night, assailed with business even when eating his food, he continually refuelled his energy from the drive and clamour of the times. He revelled in the grand political success that he was about to win, and was sure that he was on the right track.

His experience had taught him much. He knew that the British were seriously contemplating their political withdrawal. But he also knew that they would try to leave Ghana in a condition where the old regional divisions of the colonial period, and the men of substance who wanted those divisions to continue, would conserve a large influence on the country's future. In this way a self-governing Ghana would remain a suitably dependent part of the same economic system as before.

His aim, therefore, was to end the compromise as soon as possible, but to end it with the C.P.P. in power. Only in this way could the fruits of the compromise, of 'tactful action' and all its tactical retreats, be realized at last, and the way be opened for 'strategic action' which need not be tactful but could lead boldly towards unity and social change. If radical action after independence seemed farther than ever from his thoughts, the appearance was misleading. He kept his convictions to himself. But he did not give them up.

This was more than could be said for some of his colleagues who had previously shared these convictions about unity and progress. Several had already managed to 'find the cash' to build big houses; others were busy at the same interesting task; and the size of a man's motor car was beginning to be the measure of his social prestige. Yet Nkrumah said little on the subject. He had to keep the party together while it made its great effort for supremacy in an independent state. It seemed no time for the raging rows and splits that must have followed any attempt inside the party leadership to swing back from the right.

After the Motion of Destiny, the British agreed to a new general election, and this, they promised, would in turn lead to an all-African cabinet with responsibility to an all-African parliament. The election was fixed for June 1954.

The rush for places at once became a general one. It was somewhat like the opening of the gates at a famous football match, with prizes for all who could elbow their way into a seat. Nothing showed more dramatically how fragile were the party's unity and sense of common purpose. The situation demanded a maximum of both, so as to give the C.P.P. its greatest possible strength and thus clear the way for policies of genuine social change. Instead, the electoral campaign became a battle of conflicting interests. This was a fight among parties. There were seven of these by now, as well as the C.P.P. and its main opponent, the Ghana Congress Party of Dr Busia and the men of substance. But it was also a fight between regions and even between villages.

It was not surprising. The 1954 election, as Dennis Austin has remarked, was 'the first country-wide election to be held by direct ballot in single-member, territorial constituencies'. That would have been all right if the C.P.P. had been able to promote a strong sense of national consciousness. As it was, local rivalries rose quickly to the surface.

A seat in the new assembly, again in Austin's words, was seen as 'source of pride to a district. It also carried with it the hope of material benefits, not only for the successful candidate, but for the particular district in which he was born. For to have one's own village candidate elected could affect the siting of a local court, a district council headquarters, a new school, a borehole, a power station. In short, a candidate was an investment, and the dividends could be high.'*

Nkrumah needed the greatest concentration and discipline of the C.P.P.'s national effort. He found the party now assailed by a multitude of local rivalries. Out of a total of 323 competitors who inscribed themselves as candidates in the election, no fewer than 160 were 'independents'. Of these independents, more than half were members of the C.P.P. prepared to stand against official C.P.P. candidates.

He was disappointed, but also angry. 'I discovered,' he wrote later, 'that 81 party members had put themselves up to stand against official candidates. I called these people "rebels". Firm action had to be taken . . . I therefore called a meeting at Kumasi and, feeling rather as an executioner must do when he has to carry out his distasteful job because of duty and justice, I expelled each of the 81 "rebels" from the Party.'

After this the C.P.P. went into the election with 104 candidates, or one in each constituency. Their campaign became known as 'Operation 104', and its slogans were as simple as its programme: 'Vote C.P.P. to Complete the Job', and 'Forward with the Common People'.

'The torch of independence now rests in your hands,' declared Nkrumah's manifesto:

It now depends on the broad masses of people in this country, by voting into power a national movement committed to the achievement of independence by advanced political strategy, to shorten the transition between the proclamation of full internal self-government and complete independence within the Commonwealth of Nations.

It spoke proudly of the C.P.P.'s achievements even within the narrow limits of the compromise of 1951. The C.P.P. government had abolished fees for primary education; this 'has doubled the school population in two years'. Higher education had gone

* D. Austin, *Politics in Ghana 1946–60*, London, 1964, p. 211.

ahead with the expansion of the University college at Legon and the launching of a college of technology at Kumasi. 'In all these fields more has been done [by this government] under its leader Kwame Nkrumah than by any previous government.' It was perfectly true.

'But the semi-C.P.P. government'—'semi' because the British were still in final control—'has done more. The outlook of our people has changed out of recognition. A spirit of liberty, of national consciousness, pervades the country, and the *Common People* have come to feel that they are as good as the so-called aristocrats who have ignored and despised them.' And this, again, was true.

Just how profoundly true it was can be grasped, perhaps, only by those who knew Africa in the time of full colonialism. If the peoples of this country had never lacked confidence in their own value, it was still the fact that the last three years had given them a pride and sense of purpose that were new. They had gone far to recover a sense of command of their own lives, of their own history, of their own future. Ghana's name stood high in every part of the colonial world. And its leaders, not unjustly, saw themselves at the head of a continental movement of resurgence.

There were those who saw things differently. The leaders of the opposition were still furious at past successes of the C.P.P., and alarmed by the prospect of future ones. They appealed to London to prevent any such disaster. They backed up these appeals by bitter attacks in local newspapers. They did whatever they could to show that the road to independence must be a road to ruin unless it was they, the chiefs and men of substance, who led along it.

The election proved a brilliant affair, even a rather gay one. Flags and party symbols fluttered in towns and villages. Flourished on countless banners of white cotton, the red cockerel of the C.P.P. was rivalled by the Congress Party's blue elephant, the Northern Peoples' clenched fist which had nothing to do with communism, and many other pictorial statements of strength and purpose. Some of the most instructive symbols were those of the various independent groups, such as a cooking pot in one case and a grand yellow Jaguar car in another. All this was coupled with a flood of oratory. Ghanaians give ground to nobody in that particular art. They exercised it now with a more than usual energy.

Observers reported that the electoral administration was admirably sound. Efficiently, it gathered in the votes. This caused some surprise in Britain and other European countries. It was commonly believed that Africans knew nothing about representative methods of self-rule; and there was much alarm that Britain should thus permit Africans to have a one-man-one-vote election. But as soon became clear, it was the crudity of the imported institutions of parliamentary rule, not African incapacity, that opened the gate to their eventual frustration.

Ghana's own systems of self-rule, like many of those of black Africa, had been based on one great central principle, however often defied in practice: on the distrust of power. Even in the highly centralized Ashanti Empire, the exercise of power was subject to inbuilt 'checks and balances'; and every chief who was appointed to wield power was subject to complex cere-monies designed to clip his chances of misusing it.

The 'Westminster system' cut through all that with an arrogantly reckless hand. That was all to the good from Nkrumah's point of view, in so far as it reduced the power of conservative kings and their henchmen. But it was all to the bad in that it also beckoned to every sort of rivalry and con-flict, whether individual, ethnic or commercial. In these circum-stances only a great extension of democracy, only a party of active mass participation at every level of its organization, could have now prevented the abuse of power; but there was no such party on the scene. The imported institutions of parliamentary rule became, in consequence, a guarantee of divisive conflict and personal ambition.

These elections were honestly carried through, and set the scene in good ways and in bad for all that followed. Nkrumah's immediate triumph was overwhelming. The C.P.P. won 72 seats out of 104. Beyond anyone's contesting, it became not only the party of government once more, but also the party of imminent independence. The party of the men of substance gained only 2·9 per cent of the total poll; Busia alone won a seat for it, and this by only eleven votes. Danquah failed by a margin of more than 1,200 votes in a constituency poll of about 8,500. Even in Ashanti the C.P.P. won eighteen seats out of twenty-one. Only in the Northern Territories, still the electoral fief of local chiefs and other regional interests, was the C.P.P. defeated, winning eight seats against the Northern Peoples' Party's fifteen seats.

But this was not the whole story. The C.P.P. won comparatively far more seats than votes, thanks to the British system of 'straight majority' election. Thus the C.P.P. scored only 391,817 votes against a total of 314,903 for all the opposition parties, or 55·4 per cent against 44·6 per cent. The electoral victory was enough to ensure further and rapid progress to independence, but it was not enough to overcome the divisive conflicts now on stage.

The unity of the C.P.P. as a national party was opposed by a scatter of opposition parties whose interests were mainly local or regional. This had the effect of dragging down the C.P.P. to the opposition level: its candidates, more and more, were themselves obliged to think in terms of local rather than national interests. Many of them were doing that anyway. The tendency now became stronger, but less excusable.

If Nkrumah had been a run-of-the-road political boss, concerned only with hanging on to power, he could have continually 'worked his own interest' by playing off rivals against each other. This is what he was obliged to do in his last years, but he did not do it now. He continually raised the whole level of political action and argument, pointing to the future, arguing the cause of unity and progress and all it could achieve. He wanted independence for Ghana because he found the compromise offensive, but also because, once independent, Ghana could lead the way to continental strength. These were hard years, but for him they were also good years.

Rather than welcoming local intrigue and regional conflict, as a means of ensuring himself an easy life at the head of a neo-colonial system, he could not bear their petty bickering and provincialism. Yet he had to work with it to some extent, for there was no other way forward. It was clear that the new election must in any case open a period of regional struggle, sharp and possibly violent; and he braced himself for its impact. The struggle was not long in starting. Soon it became so sharp as to threaten all his plans.

HEART OF THE TROUBLE

The trouble was not centred in the Northern Territories, where the C.P.P. had lost. Just because they had lost there, perhaps the position was easier for them in the north. In line with African tradition, they needed only to find a way of drawing the leaders of the Northern Peoples' Party into an agreement. This was substantially achieved over the next year or so.

Nor was there any great trouble in the areas of the 'Colony proper', along the coast. Here the C.P.P. carried 178,000 votes out of 265,000, and 38 seats out of 45. The setback came in Ashanti, and there it was bad.

In Ashanti the C.P.P. won 95,000 votes to the disunited opposition's 65,000. But the real situation was much less favourable. More than a fifth of all the votes had gone to C.P.P. rebels, expelled by Nkrumah from the C.P.P., who had persisted in their candidatures. So it came about, at this most critical time in the nation's birth, that the 'traditional opposition' of the chiefs and men of substance, and other local separatists, was combined with the opposition of commoners; and of commoners who spoke the mind of a great many ordinary people. They spoke, above all, about cocoa.

Ashanti produced nearly half Ghana's cocoa. Great numbers of people there depended on it for their livelihood. The price of cocoa was the thing they had most to care about. Fred Sarpong, an opposition journalist, wittily explained why, in a 'high life' song which became widely popular:

> If you want to send your children to school, it is cocoa,
> If you want to build your house, it is cocoa,
> If you want to marry, it is cocoa . . .
> Whatever you want to do in this world,
> It is with cocoa money that you do it.*

Would there be more cocoa money? That was the central issue. A long-smouldering sense of worry and injustice gave it a bitter edge. Much of this came from the colonial history of rural debt.

Nkrumah and the C.P.P. ministers had learned something about cocoa problems since first looking into the files in 1951. Farmers' debt in Ashanti and other cocoa areas was clearly one of the country's big problems. It came not so much from land shortage causing high rentals, but from the absence of any effective 'credit institutions'. Nobody in the colonial period had thought to provide these, it being quite mistakenly assumed that most farmers were 'subsistence producers', producing for their own needs, and not 'cash producers'. But cocoa was a cash crop; in fact, it called for a cash investment. There being no other way of getting this capital, farmers 'pledged' their land and prospective crops in exchange for loans of ready money. The interest charged by lenders was often high, and sometimes crippling. Over the years, farmers' debts became chronic. Many suffered, above all in years when the price was low.

Colonial governors had pondered the problem. In 1948 a commission recommended the founding of a Cocoa Bank to make approved loans at the unprecedently low rate of three per cent. Nothing came of it. In 1950 the governor introduced an Agricultural Loans Board. Almost nothing came of that either. By 1952, about 70,000 farmers had asked for loans totalling some £50 millions. When suspended a year later, the Board had made exactly two loans; they totalled £1,320.

* Translated from Twi by D. Austin, *Politics in Ghana 1946–60*, London, 1964, p. 275.

Able now to know such facts, Nkrumah succeeded in getting agreement for the launching of a Cocoa Purchasing Company qualified to loan money to farmers. Within a few months this company had loaned about one million pounds, a notable advance towards the relief of debt when compared with anything done before. More than that, it helped in a new C.P.P. campaign against the 'swollen shoot' disease which was ravaging the country's cocoa farms. Colonial officials had altogether failed to persuade farmers to take the only possible action that could overcome this disease: the cutting out of infected trees, even while these trees could still bear fruit. Now this changed. Cocoa production never ceased to rise throughout Nkrumah's leadership.

Much ink was spilt by the opposition in deriding the efforts of the Cocoa Purchasing Company. Wasn't it just another honeypot for C.P.P. bureaucrats and politicians? In a small way, at least, it seems to have been that. Yet it lent farmers a million pounds in 1953, at a very low rate of interest, and other large sums later. Not fifty years of colonial rule had provided them with even a small part of such relief.

This eased things. Then the government's prospect of gaining some control of its savings in London, in the sterling reserves, appeared to promise further relief. All that now seemed necessary was to go back to the original idea of the Cocoa Marketing Board. Let the reserves, or some of them, be used to give the farmers a price somewhat nearer to the 'world price'.

It seemed obvious. The 'world price' had been steadily rising, helped upward by the consequences of 'swollen shoot'. Yet farmers had not gained. In 1951–52 they had received an average price of 80 shillings a load. A year later they received 70 shillings a load, and 72 shillings a year later again. Yet everyone knew that the 'world price' was vastly higher: in 1954, in fact, it was somewhere around 144 shillings a load, or double the price received by the farmers who grew it.

Surely there could be some improvement? Everyone in the cocoa areas thought so, and each of the parties promised that there would be. The election came and went. And almost the first of the new C.P.P. government's actions was to bring in a parliamentary measure which fixed the farmers' price, for another four years, at its *existing* level of 72 shillings.

Great discontent and anger followed, and they were well founded. The poor and humble among the farmers, precisely those whose support was most vital to the political health of the C.P.P., were those who suffered worst. Their anger fed the bitterness of the campaign of violent opposition, led by those who were neither poor nor humble, in the years that now followed. Later, after this opposition was quelled, the C.P.P.'s persistence in the same cocoa-price policy led to a growing indifference to the fortunes of the C.P.P. in general, and of Nkrumah in particular.

This refusal to improve the cocoa price in 1954, and the C.P.P.'s later persistence in the same policy, may thus be seen as a major source of rural disillusionment with the C.P.P. as a party of the masses. It ran directly counter to all that Nkrumah believed about social justice, as well as to what the C.P.P. was supposed to stand for in that field; and from this standpoint it was undoubtedly a major blunder. Yet in trying to explain it, one must also see what arguments were in play.

These were still the years of full-blooded compromise in the spirit of 1951–52. C.P.P. ministers and their advisers, so far as available records show, all thought it wise and even necessary to hold the cocoa price to its existing level. Immediately, it would help to check inflation: there was something in this, of course, though not enough to explain why *no* improvement could be made. Beyond that, however, holding down the price would reassure foreign bankers and investors: it would demonstrate the C.P.P.'s government's 'responsibility'. No less usefully, they further argued, it would conserve the country's capital and thus encourage a policy of growth.

Applied all over colonial and ex-colonial Africa with much the same results, the idea behind this policy of growth was a simple one: 'more' must be 'better'. But 'more' for whom? In Ghana's case, far from unique, a lion's share of the 'more' was going regularly abroad in one kind of capital transfer or another, direct or indirect. Making *this* economic system grow therefore meant making it still more dependent on foreign partners who already had the upper hand. This in turn meant an ever-growing dependence not only on foreign markets, but also on imports from foreign countries. And that brought an ever-rising volume of indebtedness to foreign countries. Short-term gains could derive from this policy of growth; but they would have to be paid for by long-term losses.

The proof came after Nkrumah's overthrow. It came especially in the early days of the regime installed by Colonel Acheampong. At the beginning of 1972, this regime overthrew the Busia regime which had followed on the military regime which had ousted Nkrumah. It was then revealed that the debts accumulated *since* Nkrumah's overthrow were even larger than the total of the so-called 'Nkrumah debts'.* The situation was now so bad that Ghana was having to use much of its yearly earnings only to pay the interest on these *new* debts. The policy of growth had merely reproduced, but on a national scale, the hopeless conditions of farmers' debt within the Ghana of the early 1950s.

But the truth about the policy of growth was far from understood in those early years of struggle. Partly, Nkrumah and his

---

* e.g. *West Africa*, 28 January 1972, p. 87: 'Ever since the Busia regime took office, in October 1969, the Prime Minister, the Minister of Finance, and other spokesmen have blamed the debts inherited from the Nkrumah regime for much of Ghana's economic plight. Many writers abroad have taken up the story, and for a long time the figure of £500 million was freely used in discussion of these debts, *although the real figure was less than a quarter of this* . . .

'Last September [1971] Dr Busia himself, who shares responsibility for the international misconception about the scale and the consequence of the debts inherited from Dr Nkrumah, at last gave accurate figures. These debts, usually called "medium-term", came only to some £112 million. The long term debts come to some £120 million, or more than the Nkrumah debts . . . Dr Busia did not give a figure for the very short-term commercial debts incurred under the post-Nkrumah government'—that is, the military regime which ousted him—'but arrears on payment of these was expected to reach some £100 millions by the end of last year . . .'

colleagues accepted this policy of growth because all their experts recommended it, and with dire warnings of disaster if it was rejected. Partly, they accepted it because they were in a hurry to modernize the country, and appear to have believed that farmers who had to pay so heavily for this modernization, from savings forced out of them, would still be satisfied by seeing all the new schools and services that cocoa money made possible. It was another example of how Nkrumah's impatience, 'wanting all his tomorrows today', undermined his judgement.

Yet there were other reasons for acceptance. In no small measure, the C.P.P. government accepted this policy of growth, with all its implications for rural discontent, because it chimed with the 'conservative business sense' of some of its most influential ministers, above all of Komlo Gbedemah.* In this sense the refusal to hoist the cocoa price, even by a modest amount, was another consequence of the swing to the right. Gbedemah was a shrewd and capable administrator, but he was also a very conservative one. And conservatives such as he had no difficulty in accepting what the experts said. On the contrary, they thoroughly agreed with it. 'Making the system bigger' was precisely what a businessman must want.

So the C.P.P. adopted a conservative and traders' economic policy at the very moment when its political and social policies spoke of the need for far-reaching change: in a wider sense, at the very moment when the continuing health of the C.P.P., as a party of democratic participation and mass representation, called for a radical approach to economic policy. Once again, the compromise exacted its painful price. The full scale of that was not to be known for several years, perhaps not until early in the 1970s. But the immediate consequences carried their warning.

Within a few weeks of the C.P.P.'s electoral victory of 1954, a new opposition party, calling itself the National Liberation Movement, had appeared upon the scene. And the N.L.M. was

* The words and application are those of Professor Edwin Munger of the California Institute of Technology, writing in a report of the American Universities' Field-Staff, 26 February 1959.

more than a coalition of chiefs and men of substance; it was also the spokesman of a host of ordinary people who, now, were angry people.

STRUGGLES FOR UNITY

Should Nkrumah have made haste more slowly? Wasn't it now, in these last years of the struggle for independence, that the C.P.P. lost its living contact with wage-earners in the towns and cocoa farmers in the country? Nkrumah's eyes were on distant targets, calculating long-term strategy in continental terms. Weren't these the years when he began to lose touch with the realities of daily life?

They were not the questions that were put to him at the time. Far from that, everything seemed to urge him to make haste more quickly, and to finish the compromise of 1951 by achieving the goal of full political independence. The realities of daily life came at him from many directions. Increasingly, they came with the impact of a growing violence. The challenge of this violence was to his own position in the country, but also to the national programme of the C.P.P. Only rapid action could meet it.

This challenge was made by the dissidence of Ewe separatists in Trans-Volta. It was made by Ga malcontents in Accra itself. It was made by increasingly alarmist comment in British and other foreign newspapers. But above all it came from the heart-land of Ashanti. To the tune of Ashanti war songs and the beating of Ashanti drums, with shots into the sky crackling through the fire of inflammatory speeches, the National Liberation Movement was launched in Kumasi on 19 September 1954. Here was the real challenge, launched at the very moment when the major aims of the C.P.P. seemed within grasp.

The British had accepted the results of the election as proof of the C.P.P.'s supremacy. They were ready to concede an all-African government and an all-African parliament. They were even ready for independence. But they were grudgingly ready for it. They regretted the failure of the men of substance. Knowing this, the men of substance rallied their ranks and redoubled their agitations. Would the N.L.M. now somehow rob the C.P.P. of the fruits of its work? If so, in Nkrumah's conviction, independence must become a sham. The whole long enterprise would have ended in defeat.

Before the middle of October the fifty-three chiefs of the Ashanti State Council swore by their Great Oath, the most solemn pledge they could offer, to 'give the [National Liberation] Movement their maximum support'. The sum of £20,000 was to be donated to it from the king of Ashanti's 'New Palace Building Fund'; a sum of £19,000 was actually transferred to the N.L.M. from this regular source of royal patronage. The tone was set. The N.L.M. was to enter a campaign designed for 'the stamping out of dictatorship and communistic practices'. And this at a time, be it noted, when the C.P.P. government was in its most conservative phase, and had just proved it by refusing to raise the cocoa price.

All this, in practice, meant renewed pressure for the effective separation of Ashanti from the southern part of the country where the 'dictatorship and communistic practices' of the C.P.P., duly supported by the British, now held sway. The Ashanti State Council proceeded to vote an unanimous resolution to the Queen, praying for a Royal Commission which should devise 'a federal constitution for the Gold Coast'. To this and other aims of the N.L.M. the king of Ashanti now gave his public and personal assurance of support.

It seems likely that this alarmed Nkrumah even more than the activities of the N.L.M. itself. If political independence were to come in the form of a strongly regionalized constitution, depriving the central government of effective power over two-thirds of the country, then Ghanaian independence would at once be at the mercy of 'tribal' conflict. Yet the Ashanti challenge must in any case have forced him to the strongest possible action in favour of a unitary state and constitution. This was because violence on opposition Ashanti initiative broke out almost straight away.

Violence continued on a rising scale. For many months before the final showdown, in 1956, the positions of the C.P.P. were repeatedly challenged by this opposition violence, foreshadowing the opposition terrorism of later years. Led by the robustly confident Krobo Edusei, the C.P.P. in Ashanti replied in kind. Both sides suffered much in the result; Krobo Edusei, for example, lost his own sister in the fighting. But gradually the C.P.P. men got the upper hand, thanks largely to the support of chiefs and people in Brong country peripheral to the Ashanti heartland.

Nigeria was afterwards to show, in a far more costly way, what could happen to a country gripped by the rivalries of regionalism. It was bad enough in Ghana. The most outrageous accusations became the verbal currency of the time. Goaded by fear and anger, each side let fly with anything it had, and even with a lot it did not have. Thus at one point, towards the end, the C.P.P. *Evening News* denounced 'a secret meeting recently under the chairmanship of the Asantehene', the king of Ashanti, at which the N.L.M. decided 'to get rid of Kwame Nkrumah and if necessary [Governor] Sir Charles Arden-Clarke'. Warming to its theme, the paper warned that 'if anything happens to harm either Kwame Nkrumah or Sir Charles Arden-Clarke, death will be too merciful for this gang of traitors . . .'

Violence continued in Ashanti, rising now to a climax of disorder and then dying down only to burst forth afresh. The essence of these turbulent years is that Nkrumah's leadership held the country together and completed its struggle for the country's independence. But it proved a close-run thing. Marking the violence, the British were having second thoughts. Need they really acknowledge the supremacy of the C.P.P., and meet C.P.P. demands? If so, would it not be better to make sure that the men of the N.L.M. were in any case assured of strong political ground? What the N.L.M. wanted, as they would again make clear in 1956, was a constitution by which strong regions, and above all Ashanti, would be able to dominate the central government; it was exactly the recipe that afterwards plunged Nigeria into civil war.

Nkrumah had no doubts about the disastrous nature of this recipe. His notion of the national interest, so much more constructive than that of his regionalist opponents, called for a constitution in which the central government held all the ultimate power. But he had to play for British agreement against the background of Ashanti violence. He had to accept a constitution with autonomous regions, but managed to make these much weaker than the N.L.M. desired. A constitutional adviser sent from London fortunately agreed with him.

Yet London hesitated. Going back on its earlier promise of 1953, when it had said that a C.P.P. electoral victory must clear the way for independence under a C.P.P. government, London now insisted on yet another election. Nkrumah and his ministers were more than alarmed by this. They had little doubt but that the C.P.P. could repeat in 1956 its electoral victory of 1954. But could they repeat it without another wave of violence? The answer seemed doubtful; yet a violent election would be just what could best give the British a further excuse for delay. And delay, now, could only build up disappointment and demoralization: could only threaten nationalist disarray.

They had to yield. London would not budge, handing down its final decision in May 1956. 'I have told Dr Nkrumah,' Colonial Secretary Lennox-Boyd then told the House of Commons, 'that if a general election is held, Her Majesty's Government will be ready to accept a motion calling for independence within the Commonwealth passed by a reasonable majority in the newly-elected Legislature, and then to declare a firm date for this purpose.'

An election being unavoidable, the parties girded for the fight. Meanwhile there came some helpful news from the eastern 'trust territory' of Trans-Volta, formerly part of German Togo. In May 1956 its population voted in a referendum held under United Nations auspices. They were asked to choose between union with an independent Gold Coast, and separation on some other basis. What this other basis could be was far from clear, but presumably it meant joining neighbouring Togo. As it was, a majority in northern Trans-Volta voted for union, while the Ewe majority in southern Trans-Volta voted against union. But the overall result, which is what counted, gave a fair majority for union: 96,000 votes in favour, 61,000 votes against.

The 1956 election followed in that July. As in 1954, it was preceded by a tremendous verbal barrage of abuse by the opposition, to which the C.P.P. replied in customary good measure. Speaking for the N.L.M., Dr Busia again declared in Ghana what he had often urged in London. He said that 'victory for the C.P.P. would be a national disaster'. His press went further. 'If there is any notorious liar in this country,' wrote the opposition organ, *The Liberator*, 'whose word should never, never be trusted, that man is Mr Kwame Nkrumah, one man and one man alone, the arch exponent of democratic centralism . . .' Replying some days later, the *Evening News* observed that 'the whole country had been witness to the fact that the N.L.M. and allies are unrepentant devils and brutes who are merely out to ruin the future of Ghana'. It was a high day for horrible words. If nobody took them very seriously, they too were still to have their divisive effect in the years ahead.

The violence had sporadically continued, but the actual election was generally peaceful. Its result was much as before. The C.P.P. won 71 seats out of 104 in a total poll of about the same size; out of this total poll the C.P.P. gained 57 per cent of the votes. They lost in the Ashanti heartland, where they won only 36 per cent of the votes. But to counter-balance this they were given a majority in the Brong region of the Ashanti periphery; there they carried 61 per cent of the votes.

In the circumstances it was a notable success. Now, beyond any further possible doubt, the C.P.P. had the 'reasonable majority' upon which London had insisted. Nkrumah had good grounds for satisfaction, and all the more because the regionalism under which he would now be forced to accept independence was only a weak one. He would be able to make the central government capable of ruling the whole country, and thus reduce the effects of 'tribalism'.

The opposition were far from satisfied, but had to accept. 'We are prepared', said Busia in February 1957, 'to co-operate to make' the independence constitution now devised by London 'a successful foundation for the democratic life which we all desire to see established and practised in this country (*hear hear*) . . .' To this polite murmur of *hear hears*, history took its course. But there were those, as would soon be shown, who said *hear hear* and did not mean it, or did not say it at all.

For the moment they were quiet, and this moment had its overwhelming power and influence. 'Her Majesty's Government,' Nkrumah announced, 'intends that full independence should come about on 6 March 1957.' The whole assembly, he later recalled without exaggeration, 'was for a few seconds dumb-founded. Then all at once the almost sacred silence was broken by an ear-splitting cheer . . . Some were too deeply moved to control their tears, among them some of my closer associates, those who had really felt the brunt of the battle . . .'

For Africans, at least, it was one of the decisive episodes of modern times: the dividing point, more than symbolically, between colonial past and independent future. At last the mountain of foreign rule was being thrust aside. They carried him shoulder-high into the streets, and people danced with their delight. Historian that he was, he did not fail to note that independence would fall on the anniversary of the Fanti Bond, the coastal agreement of 1844 by which the British had laid the foundations of their colonial rule. It would be the 113th anniversary. The road to freedom had been a long one.

DANCING DAYS

There are many photographs of him in those days of happiness, and many memories. Now that the British were going, let them go in peace: he did his best to make it so. He knew that he had won, but he also knew the British style. He had made it very much his own, which is another reason why Governor Arden-Clarke will also have his place in history.

After the election, on 23 August, he duly asked for Britain's formal consent to independence. It came on 17 September. That day, he wrote in his deliberately 'tactful' autobiography,

I had a full morning's work ahead of me and I was going over my diary of appointments. Suddenly there was a ring from the telephone that connected me direct with the Governor.

'Good morning, P.M.,' said Sir Charles: 'I just wanted to tell you that I have received some good news for you. I wondered if you could come up and see me for a few minutes when you are free.'

'Yes, certainly, Sir Charles,' I said, as I hurriedly scanned through my appointments. 'I'm afraid this morning is pretty hectic—would three o'clock this afternoon be all right?'

Not very surprisingly it was 'all right', and the good news was duly handed over with mutual congratulations between the two men who had made it possible. They had opened their compromise six years earlier in doubt and suspicion, and had come to trust each other. But which of them had got the better of the bargain?

Each had reason for satisfaction. Arden-Clarke had presided over the birth of an African political freedom, by any measure a momentous one, which seemed to guarantee 'continuity' with the colonial system. It would afterwards be shown that this 'continuity' must be fatal to a genuine independence. But that is not how the Governor saw it, or, given his convictions, could have seen it. For him, as for most British well-wishers, independence within the framework of existing institutions, British-exampled institutions, was the best there could be.

Nkrumah had no belief in the value of any such 'continuity'. Yet he too, at long last, had got the substance of what he wanted: the power to break that 'continuity', to give Ghanaians the command of their own history and to reshape their future as they themselves thought best. If this appeared in his mind as being how he thought best, there were at least no other serious contenders on the scene.

For the moment, though, everything must still depend on his tactical skill. A promise was a promise, but it might still be broken or at least delayed. The constitution was far from satisfactory; its regionalism could still open the way to a renewal of separatist violence. That would have to be prevented. But it could not be prevented until the British had signed on the dotted line. Ticklish days lay ahead. Nkrumah entered on his most tactful phase of 'tactical action'. He abounded in polite and reassuring words and gestures.

They were rewarded. There now came all that had been missing in 1951; above all, the recognition of the world. Visitors poured in. Congratulations arrived in floods of telegrams and letters. Even the opposition, astonished by its own mixed feelings of regretful pride, was temporarily disarmed. Even hostile newspapers in London held their fire.

Independence was celebrated with every brilliance that could illustrate its historical importance. It happened on 6 March. He was forty-seven.

The fact that he was forty-seven was not so easy to remember. Tireless, enthusiastic, bubbling with ideas, he seemed far less. And his seeming far less, as I remember, was constantly reinforced by the sheer youthfulness of the whole situation. Ghana was really a very old country, deeply set in its ways; but in those weeks it seemed an altogether youthful country with everything to do and to be. All sorts of people were aspiring to work and responsibilities they had never before been allowed to perform or assume, had perhaps never before thought they could perform or assume. New careers were soaring away by the hundred. It was a very 'young' atmosphere, and Nkrumah was at the heart of it.

One of his first gestures made the point. He threw a tea party for Accra children. Hundreds came, toddling or running about the watered lawns beside his ministerial office. He hadn't been a schoolmaster for nothing. He closed the tea party with an announcement of a day's school holiday, and then went off to a broadcasting station to tell the country that it was now an independent nation.

All the same, he was forty-seven; and the fact was important.

Not because he had lost any of his capacity for work, but because he too, like his country, was set in his character and attitudes, and formed in his beliefs and ideas. As before, as in 1951, there was the same distance between his intentions and those of most of his colleagues. The testing years had developed him, had greatly enlarged his practical experience; but they had not really changed him. He was still the visionary who had come back over the Atlantic, in 1945, peering ahead for the route to black unity and strength. He had lost none of his belief in his continental mission, none of his determination to see immediate gains only as steps to other and still more difficult gains. If anything, the testing years had reinforced his missionary belief, for they had nourished it with success. This increased his self-confidence. It also increased his impatience.

He still lived simply, enjoying personal comforts but making no great fuss about them. Among a people greatly given to the enjoyment of life, he remained something of an ascetic. This did nothing to prevent new clouds of gossip, especially in Accra where gossip now became a positive addiction, about the immorality and lavishness of his private life. Some of it, no doubt, was well enough founded; much of it, by all the evidence, was sheer invention. Just as in the past, he gave his confidence rarely, fearing emotional involvement. Friends whom he trusted say that he could be gay and easy-going. He greatly depended on these friends. Often, after 1957, they were not Ghanaians.

A certain loneliness was setting in, helped on by the increasingly factional nature of the C.P.P. political machine. This loneliness was deepened by the cult of his personality which eager voices had helped to build around him. If Nkrumah was proclaimed as 'untouchable', then down the scale so would others be. He let this cult grow, a little sarcastically at first; and then, with time, allowing it to take its course and even helping it to do so. How otherwise control the factions, how otherwise conserve his vision of the nation's future, and himself as its symbol? With all his qualities he still remained a man of his place and period. When the Assembly proposed to erect a statue of him outside their doors, he was more than pleased.

Partly, he thought the cult useful. Even some of his radical supporters, after 1961, saw this cult as a 'charismatic instrument' for the building of unity. He also believed that his judgement was unswayed by it. He had been right in the past: wasn't he right now? Increasingly, he failed to check the more absurd and offensive manifestations of an adulation that was increasingly false. But for a while it did little harm beyond offending many who wished him well, and infuriating many who did not.

He believed more than ever in his own destiny. The black star of Ghana's liberation was to be no mere national guide. Published in those dancing days of 1957, the last words of his autobiography gave the tone that he meant to hold.

I have never regarded the struggle for independence of the Gold Coast as an isolated objective but always as a part of a general world historical pattern . . .

As a ship that has been freshly launched we face the hazards of the high seas alone. We must rely on our own men, on the captain and his navigation. And, as I proudly stand on the bridge of that lone vessel as she confidently sets sail, I raise a hand to shade my eyes from the glaring African sun, and scan the horizon. There is so much more beyond.

The compromise of 1951, with all its twists and turns and worrying retreats, had been made to yield its harvest. Many had doubted its value, himself among them. He told the Assembly in November 1956:

When I first became Prime Minister I determined that I would compromise, if necessary, on every issue except one—the independence of this country.

In consequence I have had from time to time to give way on this or that point, and even to persuade my Party to accept half-measures which we all knew in our hearts were basically unsatisfactory. This policy of which I, at times, had grave doubts, has proved successful.

Who could doubt it now? Its maker and his colleagues sat in the seats of power. His name, and Ghana's, were becoming famous round the world. As Ghana's leader he was now to be the guest of kings and presidents. The Queen in London would appoint him to her Most Honourable Privy Council, and he would stay at the royal castle of Balmoral. No black man had ever before been given this kind of respect. He saw it as a tribute to himself, but also as a tribute to black people everywhere.

Many thought that he would rest content with the harvest as it was, and break no more new ground. Already, for them, he had broken quite enough ground. On independence day in Accra the European club, still for whites only, held more than a few members who sipped their gins in irritated silence and shook their heads at the antics of the natives, and above all the top native. The ground that he had already broken was more than enough for them. But while they were shaking their heads, the people outside on the bare-ground esplanades were shaking their feet.

In the evening of that famous Day of Independence, with Botsio and Gbedemah and other veterans, he went to receive their cheers. It was a moment that really seemed to strike the knell of the old world of colonial silence. As the sun went down in glittering phosphorescence along the line of ocean surf, a whole wide plain was swaying with the rhythm of a multitude, their drums thudding in the night, their voices singing the songs of yesterday but also the songs of tomorrow.

He had no intention of resting content with the harvest as it was. Those who believed that he would were making the same mistake as the U.G.C.C. leaders, back in 1947. Other leaders in the near future might be well enough satisfied with the songs and flags of sovereignty. That was not going to be his way.

It was March 1957. Far in the north, the flames of colonial war engulfed Algeria. Elsewhere the cause of change swung uncertainly between advance and defeat. Not for another year and a half could a second black colony follow Ghana's lead.

4. Victor and Victim

Something in the nature of an economic revolution
is required.

Nkrumah, 'Neo-Colonialism'

TOWARDS UNITY AND PROGRESS

After his ten-year struggle for power, there followed a nine-year
use of power. This nine-year period after 1957 was one of
deepening drama as new problems took the place of old. It was
also one of considerable fulfilment, and the period when Nkrumah
acquired his world-wide reputation, assured himself of a high
place in modern African history, and, in step with that, also
multiplied his enemies and critics at home and abroad.

If much of this short book has concerned itself with the years
before 1957, the years before independence, this is because these
years, at least in the writer's view, shaped all the groundwork
and achievement of his life, bringing his great success but also
preparing his downfall. No one can understand the nature of
the Nkrumah regime's ultimate failure without having understood the nature of its initial triumph. What happened after
1957, and what *could* happen then, were continually and closely
governed by what had gone before. Independence brought no
sharp break with the past, even though some appearances might
suggest the contrary.

The success was great in many fields of life, whether inside
Ghana or outside. Social services could be continually enlarged
and improved. A constructive modernization could appear in
many different guises. In some of the more obvious of these,
the country began to produce its own engineers, scientists, and
technicians with a wide variety of skills. And as Nkrumah's
Ghana led the way for black men and women to speak as equals

in the councils of the world, and the world began to listen as they spoke, the dignity of Africans began to have a new and modern meaning.

The fruits of the years of compromise of 1951–57 were reaped in generous measure. Already in those years, for example, the C.P.P. in office had presided over the building of nine new hospitals, and had enlarged and modernized fifteen others. These the country had sorely needed; yet it was only a start. Whether in the period of 'continued compromise' between independence in 1957 and the declaration of the Republic in 1960, or after 1960, Ghana advanced towards the possession of a medical service of her own, its formative organization being eventually crowned by a teaching hospital where the country's own doctors could be trained.

A truly independent country, unlike a colony or a 'neo-colony', must be able to ensure its social and cultural progress from its own reserves of human energy and talent. In Ghana these reserves began to be widely used, above all in the field of the people's education, for Aggrey's old pupil required no telling that the road to liberation lay through knowledge.

Here, too, the efforts made before 1957 were carried forward after independence. They had lain and continued to lie in three 'spheres': those of organization, quantity of pupils, and quality of instruction. Aiming at this national system of education, the nationalists in office had taken their first big step in 1952. As many as 1,400 private schools were then brought within the public system in order to improve and supervise their effort. This work of unification continued. In 1961 the government was far enough advanced to make primary education compulsory as well as free. Steps were taken at the same time to train many more teachers. This effort went forward at a quickening pace as teacher-trainees began to come in quantity from new secondary schools and universities. So it was that by 1965 there were to be forty-four teachers' training colleges; in 1966, the year of Nkrumah's overthrow, many more were ready to open.

For the first time, a real attention was paid to technical and artisan types of education suited to a country which would have to pull itself up, as Nkrumah never tired of saying, by its own shoe-laces. Even by 1957, thanks to the pressures exercised by the C.P.P. while in office since 1951, the number of primary schools had expanded beyond 3,000; and there were 931 middle schools and thirty-eight secondary schools, many more than before 1951. By 1964 the number of children in primary school was to be nearly seven times greater than in 1950; the number in middle school nearly four times greater; and the number in secondary school about ten times greater.

Higher education was to show the same expansion. The old college at Achimota became a fully-fledged university at nearby Legon; a new university with emphasis on science was launched at Kumasi; a third was also set upon its way. Numbers of students rapidly expanded. Courses became more appropriate. African languages began to be studied as degree subjects for the first time; so did African history. A new Institute of African Studies under Thomas Hodgkin attracted scholars from many other countries; its activities in research became admired where-ever African culture was studied and respected. All this was reflected in the growing competence and expertise of Ghana's civil service.

One of those who overthrew Nkrumah in 1966 would after-wards justify the military coup by claiming, among other things, that 'Nkrumah's rule had planted havoc . . . in the field of education [by] a crippling lowering of educational standards'.* Another Ghanaian, in this field no doubt better qualified to judge, would note of the Nkrumah regime's educational record that 'while a certain measure of fall in quality is probably inevitable in any crash programme of educational expansion, nothing can excuse the incredibly low depths which education touched during Nkrumah's regime'.† Nothing, a historian may be tempted to comment, can also rival the incredibly high note

---

* Col. A. A. Afrifa, *The Ghana Coup*, London, 1966; see especially Chapter 5.

† A. A. Boahen, in *The Legon Observer*, 8 November 1968.

of denigration and recrimination with which Ghanaians are accustomed—as the aftermaths of post-Nkrumah regimes have repeatedly confirmed—to assail the leaders that they overthrow. It is as though a normally hard-headed people feel it necessary at such traumatic moments to take leave of all serene analysis.*

Even so, there was still a long way to go towards a balanced national system. Country children were still disadvantaged in comparison with town children. Less than one-quarter of the fathers of sixth-form pupils, it was found in 1964, were farmers. There were many more girls at school than ever before, but they were still in small proportion to the boys. More important, the quality of teaching had failed to keep in step with the expansion of school-places. Many new and more appropriate school books were made available, enabling Ghanaian schoolchildren to learn, for example, the history of their own country and continent for the first time. Some of these books were excellent; but others were less good, and several were pedestrian, expensive and bad.

Yet the criticism of this 'quantity at the expense of quality' came also from another angle of discontent, essentially a political angle. Like other privileged groups in other lands, the 'political class' of the Ghana opposition, and those who thought as they did, had no real taste for any general kind of educational expansion. They regarded education, being in this respect just like the privileged classes of England, much more as a guarantee of privilege than as a means of national progress. There was accordingly much in their repeated harping on the 'lowering of standards' that reminded one of similar cries in England during English educational expansion after the second world war.†

One saw this with particular clarity in the matter of university

---

* Noted by Ghanaians too. Launching Ghana's *Who's Who* in February 1973, Dr Robert Gardiner remarked that 'successive regimes in Ghana since independence have been inordinately concerned in castigating their predecessors, denigrating their efforts, and indulging in unbridled character assassination': *West Africa*, 26 February 1973.

† Even more, perhaps, of the cries of dismay that greeted the beginnings of English educational expansion after the 1870s.

education. The task of higher education, in the general attitude of the intellectuals of the Ghana opposition, was to forward the interests of a small group or élite, just as this had always been the task of English universities. These too, until the 1950s, had done little but produce a small élite of the sons and daughters of England's 'political class'; and these were the people who had always run England and its satellites or oversea extensions. Ghana's men of substance and their spokesmen wanted universities on the same model. And in the 1950s, just when England was advancing beyond that model, this is what they began to get.

The English began to found new university colleges in their African colonies after the second world war. Their idea was that the time had come to promote a 'responsible class' to whom, sooner or later, they could safely hand political independence. What they did was to take the pattern of Oxford or Cambridge, the greatest of Britain's old universities, and reproduce it to some extent in Africa. They worked, as the British educationalist Sir Eric Ashby was to explain, 'in the belief that the social function of a university in Africa was to create and sustain an intellectual élite'. So they built lavish colleges and student halls in pleasant African places as far removed as possible from the sweat and strain of everyday life. And in these splendid colleges, as Sir Eric Ashby also said, the new students and their teachers became 'isolated from the life of the common people in a way which has had no parallel in England since the Middle Ages'.

This isolation seemed good to the men of substance and to most of their sons or daughters. But to Nkrumah it soon began to seem very bad. Thus formed in isolation, few of the graduates could sympathize with his national aims and policies. Even before 1960 these centres of privilege, though containing many excellent and devoted persons, had become vocal centres of dissent. By 1963 the gap between their own ideas and Nkrumah's plans for broad democracy and social change had widened to an abyss. Nkrumah tried to bridge this abyss. He also tried to get the C.P.P. to bridge it. But by this time the C.P.P., as a means of political persuasion, had become more or less totally paralysed by its own élitism. Its efforts at bridging the abyss were contemptibly misconceived, and helped only to widen it still further.

Two ideas were in collision. Nkrumah thought that universities should produce men and women who would study ordinary people's needs, and serve them. But the inner conviction of the new universities was that they should produce graduates who would step automatically into positions of command, and, from these, rule according to the 'best examples'; and the best examples, in their belief, were those of privilege and conservatism.

He was led into bitter battles, notably with imported vice-chancellors. The last of these was an Irish nationalist whom Nkrumah was convinced would surely understand the dangers of an élitist type of higher education modelled on imperialist example. But this man took his stand on the old Oxfordian principle of 'academic freedom', by now a great opposition war cry. In the circumstances, this appeared tantamount to a defence of academic privilege; and what might have marked a promising new start towards reconciliation turned into angry deadlock. The distinguished Irish nationalist sat in Legon, some fifteen miles outside Accra, and seemed quite often to identify the first with Dublin and the second with London. Nkrumah, for his part, felt himself affronted and let down.

*

In this, as in other ways, political independence took over the legacy of colonial times. The legacy was to prove heaviest of all in the field of economic policy. And it was to be economic policy that would increasingly dominate the years of Nkrumah's Republic from 1960 to 1966. Repeatedly, then, it was found that the economic system taken over from the past could not afford a vast expansion of the country's welfare.

Meanwhile, the expansion was certainly impressive. A survey promoted by Ghana's newly-founded Academy of Sciences was to show this. By the last years of Nkrumah's rule, according to the Ghanaian economist E. N. Omaboe, the country achieved 'levels of social and welfare services which are in advance of those of most under-developed countries, and in some urban centres not far behind those of some developed countries'. It was a very great advance from the days when Nkrumah had first come home, and it bore witness to a national effort of memorable magnitude.

All this marked progress, even if sometimes an erratic one, in 'the liberation of minds'. These were years when Ghanaians acquired a new confidence in their own value as people and kicked away the old burden of colonial inferiority. Accra became a centre of international importance. Insistently, Nkrumah projected his vision of the future: that Africa need not only follow where others led, but that Africa could also be a leader towards stability and freedom. Even in the most tactful of the 'tactful years', he had not forgotten his old objectives. As early as December 1953 he had arranged a meeting in Kumasi aimed at promoting regional unity among West African countries. Not many came from abroad, but those who did included the Nigerians Azikiwe and Aminu Kano. They called for the creation of 'a strong and truly federal [West African] state capable of protecting itself from outside invasion, and able to preserve its internal security'.

Words in the wind, perhaps; but for Nkrumah they were words in the wind of the future. An African organic unity, he was more than ever convinced, could alone make political independence worthwhile, or even make it a reality. And now, after 1957, he was able to call diplomacy to his aid. By this time there were seven other independent states, as well as white-ruled South Africa. Of these, five had much in common: Egypt, Libya, Sudan, Tunisia, Morocco. Ethiopia had long pursued an isolation of its own. Liberia had always been firmly attached to the United States.

Yet the times were changing. In April 1958 he succeeded in calling a first conference of these seven states together with Ghana. It was above all a conference 'for getting to know each other', for pushing aside the old colonial barriers to mutual understanding. It launched a secretariat and planned further meetings. It was in a real sense the 'launching pad' for the Organization of African Unity which was to emerge five years later.

He followed this in December 1958 with a conference of representatives of movements and parties in countries not yet free. This, too, was an educational experience of some value. The notion that Africans had interests of their own which ought to be discussed in African assemblies, and defended by African organizations, began to gain strength. It stood to reason that there were disagreements and failures to agree. It was obvious that the old colonial powers were still active on the scene. Unity of purpose could only have a long and difficult birth. But Nkrumah, in this field as at home, saw no reason for dismay.

Soon he was ready for another move.

INDEPENDENT REPUBLIC: BUT WHOSE?

The years after independence, after 1957, worked out the trends of previous years in the man himself, in the opposition, and in the C.P.P.

Though many still opposed the C.P.P., or were indifferent to its claims and aims, the party can be said to have entered independence with a genuine popularity. But the time of 'tactical action' had not been good for it. Especially since the swing of 1954, the leadership had tended to govern, more and more, 'from the top down': what now weighed most in its councils were the big party offices in the capital.

Internal renewal of the party's honesty and vigour was greatly needed. Nothing like this happened. The evidence suggests that there was plenty of murmuring at the base; if so, little was allowed to filter to the summit. What did filter to the summit, on the other hand, was a rising chant of meaningless praise. Increasingly unable to renew itself, the party foundered in a sea of intrigue. In a large degree, its historical role was finished.

The opposition parties were in even worse case. Like the

C.P.P., they were stiffly bureaucratic structures in so far as they had any organizational existence, and their naturally authoritarian nature was reinforced by an aversion from a parliament they could not dominate. With an attitude increasingly destructive, they often behaved as though they were determined that the C.P.P. should become the dictatorship they had always denounced. They did much to make their prediction come true; and the C.P.P. itself did the rest.

Nkrumah was part and parcel of all this, and cannot be separated from a due share of responsibility for it. But the situation could in any case yield little to personal preferences one way or the other. Bereft of effective institutions, or burdened with ineffective ones, Ghana was bound to stagger from one political crisis to another. Yet the situation had its tragedy for Nkrumah as well as for the cause of broadening democracy. Attempting to govern as a parliamentary prime minister, and then in 1960 as a parliamentary president, he had to deal with a ruling party that was fast becoming a machine shared by factions, and with an opposition which above all else longed and worked for his downfall.

To lay all this degeneration at Nkrumah's door is, of course, as silly as to suppose that he was not involved in it. The 'petty-bourgeois' nature of this particular stage of Ghana's development—of black Africa's development, since it was to be much the same elsewhere—had come home to roost, and with a vengeance. 'The overall mood was of a constant search in the corridors of power,' Ras Makonnen, one of Nkrumah's oldest collaborators has recalled, 'and it was summed up in the phrase you heard all around you: "power sweet" . . .'

Nkrumah can be criticized for much that he did or failed to do; but the underlying truth, by this time, was that he had become the victim of a situation that increasingly escaped his control, or even his influence. Trying to recover some control, he moved increasingly towards a purely personal assertion of authority, substituting his will for that of the party, just as the party had long since, by now, substituted its will for that of the voters. In all probability, this substitution was critically bad for his understanding and insight, because it tended to play upon his vanity, upon his preference for solitary meditation rather than collective criticism, and upon his growing sense of being indispensable.

All this in turn intensified the 'atmosphere of intrigue' that was now 'central to the politics of Ghana'.* But, of course, it was also a response to that atmosphere. The manipulation of factions was fast becoming Nkrumah's sole effective mode of action: his resignation could be the only other choice. Could he have seriously changed the situation by resigning and 'going to the people'? Not, so far as one can see, in any immediate sense: only long years of obscure and patient work could now build an alternative to the C.P.P. And Nkrumah had no mind at this stage for obscure and patient work. He had just laid hold of the keys of power, and meant to use them on the locks that still imprisoned Ghana in its colonial past. That was the future as he saw it now.

The opposition chiefs had said what they thought about the future in some curiously frank comments by the N.L.M. (National Liberation Movement) on the constitutional proposals of 1956, and they did not afterwards budge from it. If the British allowed Ghana to become independent under the C.P.P., they had said in 1956, this would be a road that 'as far as we can see makes for the country of riot, rebellion, revolution, the road long ago taken by those unhappy countries where one can change only the Head of State or the people who govern by armed insurrection after underground conspiracy and sabotage'.†

* With the previous quotation from Ras Makonnen, this is from *Pan-Africanism From Within*, with Kenneth King, Oxford University Press, 1973 (forthcoming): I am grateful for having been allowed to quote from these fascinating memoirs. See also p. 175.

† 'Statement by the National Liberal Movement and its Allies', Kumasi, 19 April 1956, signed by Bafuor Osei Akoto, chairman of the N.L.M.; S. D. Dombo, Douri-Na, chairman of the Northern Peoples' Party; Bankole Awooner-Renner, chairman of the Muslim Association Party; W. E. G. Sekyi, president of the Aborigines' Rights Protection Society; and S. G. Antor, secretary-general of the Togoland Congress.

The other road, perhaps needless to say, would be a constitution under their control and would lead 'to democracy and parliament'. They saw no unreality in the fact that they spoke for 'democracy' in the name of persons inured to aristocratic privilege, and claimed 'parliament' for themselves at a time when a fully-fledged parliament under C.P.P. leadership was about to open its proceedings in Accra.

Their road, in fact, was to prove a short one to conspiracy. Others, of the same mind, took an even shorter road to that end. Within a few months of independence, there emerged in Accra another ethnic party, the Ga Shifimo Kpee, the 'Standfast Association' of the Ga people whose chief centre was the capital itself. Ethnic parties being outlawed as a form of tribalism, they organized themselves as a conspiracy, complete with secret oaths and secret meetings addressed by masked speakers.

Their action wing was known as the 'Tokyo Joes'. At least the Special Branch of the police became convinced that these included a number of men with records of criminal violence; and it is worth remembering, in this connection, that the Special Branch was still commanded by a British appointee, in fact an Irishman. Its judgement may have been wrong; it was in any case not the C.P.P.'s judgement, though they certainly accepted it.

The 'Tokyo Joes' were not long in showing what they thought about 'democracy and parliament'. Three months after independence, Nkrumah returned from the first meeting of prime ministers of the British Commonwealth ever attended by an African. The constitution approved by London was in full swing. A perfectly honest general election had just returned the C.P.P. to power, and the C.P.P. was getting ready to govern according to all the rules and precedents of Westminster. But the 'Tokyo Joes' of Ga 'tribalism' met Nkrumah along the road from the airport with shouts and placards of 'Dictator'.

The police urged the use of special powers to put down this kind of abuse, and its consequent disorders that could now be feared. This was how they had always acted; it was indeed the invariable colonial answer to any such 'unrest'. Even in newly-independent India, Jawaharlal Nehru had lately introduced a Preventive Detention Act to deal with men and groups who flouted the law but whom the law, always difficult to apply in such circumstances, could not itself deal with.

Nkrumah hesitated. He knew what would be said of him if he introduced a Preventive Detention Act. It had not been said of Nehru; but Nehru was not a black man. His critics in the British Press were not saying it of Colonial Secretary Lennox-Boyd, then using the same special powers in Kenya, but he was not a black man either. Let a black man do the same, and this would be denounced as the most dastardly proof of dictatorial ambitions.

But in June 1958 the police came up with evidence of another conspiracy. The general secretary of the opposition line-up, R. R. Amponsah, was found to have bought some odds and ends of military equipment, though not weapons, in a London shop. He had used a false name, and had ordered the equipment to be sent to an accommodation address in neighbouring French Togo, still a colony. Amponsah was arrested and charged with sedition, not for doing this, but for accusing the police of helping the government to print false ballot-papers for elections then forthcoming to the regional assemblies. This accusation was shown to be baseless. Yet the court still acquitted Amponsah of sedition on the grounds that the prosecution had misconceived the charge.

In July, urged on by reactions to this acquittal, the majority in parliament passed its Preventive Detention Act. Four months later the government began to use it. Some forty members of the opposition were detained on the grounds that they were engaged in dangerous political activities, but such as the law would not be able to prove. And another month later there came the strange case of Captain Awhaitey.

In January 1959 this officer of the Ghana Army was court-martialled on the orders of the commanding general, an Englishman named Paley, and dismissed the service. The evidence against him was that he had failed to report a conspiracy against Nkrumah's life. The conspirators were named as Amponsah, the buyer of army equipment in London, and Modesto Apaloo, an opposition politician of Ewe origin, who was said to have addressed meetings of the Ga Shifimo Kpee.

Only Amponsah and Apaloo were detained, as well as Captain Awhaitey. But it was noted that not a single opposition leader uttered a word of disapproval of the action of their detained colleagues, although this action was described by a commission of impeccable credentials. Nor did a single one of them say a word in exoneration of themselves from a not unreasonable suspicion that some of them, at least, had been involved in the conspiracy found by the commission. On the contrary, Dr Kofi Busia thought it well to flee the country, passing the northern frontier in secret, while his colleagues who remained behind were content to attack the commission for its findings.

And so the scene was laid. From now onwards the opposition was to show itself ever less willing or capable of acting as a responsible parliamentary check on the C.P.P. machine; and the C.P.P. machine, duly unchecked, went recklessly upon its way.

So did the police. Sparingly at first. Yet by 1960 they had brought in sixty-three persons for political reasons; they had also brought in another 255 for gangsterism of one sort of another. All this was taken by Nkrumah's critics abroad as the work of an outright dictatorship. By 1966 the number of detentions would rise to about 800, of whom, according to such partial records as are now available, about half were detained for non-political reasons such as smuggling or assault.

Meanwhile, in between, persons largely unknown had made two separate attempts at killing Nkrumah by bombs or shooting, and caused much other violence of the same kind. Thirty people in the streets were slain by such outrages, and about 300 seriously maimed. Up to 1966, the regime executed only one terrorist, a policeman who had murdered another policeman while attempting to murder Nkrumah. Some of those in gaol suffered badly, although no worse, it afterwards appeared, than detained persons under subsequent regimes.

This is looking ahead of 1960, though only a little. By now Nkrumah was convinced that the time had come to move towards some of the social and political objectives that he had had to shelve during 'tactical action'. On the political side, this supposed a strong unitary state, as well as an expansion of popular democracy. On the economic side, reinforcing that expansion, it supposed a preliminary turning away from the traditional 'policy of growth', the capitalist-colonialist policy, towards state-capitalist policies which should, as he thought, lead to socialist policies.

His first step was to secure a republican constitution. It was offered to the electorate in a plebiscite. This gave just over one million votes in favour, and 131,425 against: or 88·5 per cent against 11·5 per cent. At the same time the country voted for its first president. The C.P.P. candidate was of course Nkrumah, the opposition's J. B. Danquah. The results were almost exactly the same: just over a million votes for Nkrumah and 124,623 for Danquah: or 89·1 per cent against 10·9 per cent. There was evidence that both sets of results were partly faked by the C.P.P. machinery and administration. Yet there can be very little doubt that an honest election would still have produced overall majorities for the republican constitution and Nkrumah as president, at least outside the Ashanti heartland and the Ga stronghold of Accra.

If with reservations on quantity, the verdict may be taken as a democratically representative one. But the question still remained: whose Republic was this to be? Was it to belong to the C.P.P. machine and all its cliques of 'beneficiaries', or was it to be an instrument for social and economic progress throughout the nation? Was it to mark a further step towards national liberation, or merely introduce another phase of compromise between the interests of men of substance abroad and men of substance at home?

THE WRITING ON THE WALL

The answer came in a series of dramatic turning points.

The Ghana government and its president were much occupied with African affairs in 1960, the year of political decolonization not only for the vast federation of Nigeria but also for the many countries of the French African empire. All this widened Ghana's possible field of action. But events in 1960 also brought fearful setbacks in the ex-Belgian Congo. Once again Nkrumah's Ghana made history, this time by sending its troops to save the independence of a brother African country. The saving failed; and this experience in the Congo, but above all the murder of the Congo leader Lumumba by Katanga separatists, seem to have formed for Nkrumah the final demonstration that policies of 'tact', of 'continuity', of conformity with Western wishes, had nothing more to offer.

He acted on this conviction; and it was from this time, especially, that foreign opponents made him their butt and target for abuse. He shrugged all that aside, and soon drew new fusillades by a policy of commercial non-alignment, leading to trade-and-aid agreements with the countries of the Soviet bloc. That sort of non-alignment has long since become an everyday affair; when Nkrumah embarked upon it, there were many in the Western world who saw it as a hostile challenge or a dastardly betrayal.

There were others who denounced it as plain proof of Soviet subversion. Today that may seem just as wide of the mark, now that nearly all African countries have commercial and diplomatic ties with the Soviet Union, China, or other countries with communist governments, but without any sensible person supposing they are therefore subject to Soviet or Chinese indirect rule. But in those days the notion of African non-alignment, of Africa's right to look for partners wherever Africa's interest might be served, was a matter for strong Western dissent; and the men of Ghana's opposition, irrespective of whatever benefits Ghana might derive from non-alignment, made the most of this.

They added fuel to the fires of even the least responsible forms of Western suspicion. So it was that Dr Kofi Busia, in exile then as afterwards, found it well and wise to travel to Washington in order to give his support to a Congress Committee presided over by the extremist Senator Dodd, and to take part in proceedings aimed at preventing any further financial aid to Ghana. This might seem a strange way of recalling Ghana to 'respectability', but Dr Busia did not see it thus: for him, apparently, the great desideratum was to ensure that America should be hostile to Ghana.

He revealed, in doing so, how little the new nation had become a focus for patriotic loyalty. Senator Dodd led off by stating that Ghana had become 'the mortal enemy of true freedom and independence for the peoples of Africa and the mortal enemy of African peace'. Dr Busia could only agree with him. 'I should say', he told the Senator, 'that politics isn't my career, but what made me go into politics is the fact that I saw right at the beginning, as far back as Nkrumah's return, back in 1948–49'—it was actually in 1947—'that we had there all the makings, all the ingredients of revolutionary communism.' Even the old men of substance of the U.G.C.C., not to speak of Governor Arden-Clarke, would have winced a little at hearing such nonsense.

Others were to wince still more. After discussing the trial then going on in Nigeria of Chief Obafemi Awolowo, in which Ghanaian subversion was alleged as part of the charge, there occurred the following exchange:

Senator Dodd: I take it that it is your opinion that Ghana is the center for subversive Communist activities in Western Africa, is that right?

Mr Busia: Mr Chairman, I have stated this many times before . . .*

* 'Is U.S. Money aiding another Communist State?' Text of a Hearing before the sub-committee to investigate the administration of the Internal Security Act etc. Committee of the Judiciary, U.S. Senate, 87th Congress, 2nd Session. Testimony of K. A. Busia, 3 December 1962, U.S. Government Printing Office.

Events have amply shown the absurdity of these opinions; the interesting point here is the light that it throws on eminent opposition spokesmen of those years. Much was done by Nkrumah to forward, or to try to forward, the cause of nationalist parties in colonies not yet free. Much was not well done; but none of it had anything remotely to do with communism, and no impartial observer ever thought that it had.

The truth is that the Ghana opposition had not the slightest use for Nkrumah's notion that Ghana's lead in gaining independence should be made of value to other Africans still under colonial rule. In this they were not even true to the liberal English tradition of which they invariably spoke with such respect. Helping other Africans, for Dr Busia, was evidently wrong and even wicked. Yet as Thomas Hodgkin would put it some years later, when discussing the same point in connection with Camerounian exiles helped by Nkrumah: 'Was it any more subversive for the government of Ghana to provide asylum for Camerounians seeking to overthrow their legitimate government than for 19th century Britain to provide asylum for Italians seeking to overthrow the government of Naples (and other lawful governments)?'[*]

One may note, in passing, that Nkrumah's trade-and-aid agreements with the Soviet bloc never led to any establishment of Soviet, or any other communist, influence in Ghana. Nor did any such increase even follow upon the sending of students to the Soviet Union. This was because the Soviet rulers, not suffering from the provincialism of the Ghana opposition, were men who understood the world they were living in. But it was also because there existed only a very narrow political ground for the infiltration of left-wing ideas, and not least among the students who 'went East'.

Most of these students were from higher education thoroughly imbued with the imperialist tradition; many were the sons of men of substance for whom a 'scholarship' in Russia was very much the second-best to a 'scholarship' almost anywhere in the

[*] T. Hodgkin, in *Venture*, London, June 1966, vol. 18, no. 5.

West. No friend of the Soviet Union, Ras Makonnen has put it this way: 'The colonial mentality was so deeply engrained that when we began to send hundreds of students to places like Russia, it was plain that they despised the Russians.' Yet this was the Ghana, that for Dr Busia, had become 'a center for subversive Communist activities'.

What Ghana had really become, as was now flagrantly clear, was a centre for subversive commercial activities among all who were in a position to indulge in them, and among several of the leaders of the C.P.P. in the first place. Nkrumah now began trying to reverse this trend.

Upbraiding the conduct of C.P.P. men in a speech of this period, he described how 'some comrades make it their habit to go around the country in a bid to get rich quick by threatening people and collecting money from them . . . a most vicious and shameful practice'. Another 'malpractice which undermines the efficiency of our Party work is the manufacture of lying propaganda against men in key positions . . . conversely, some Party members in high positions use their position to threaten and intimidate those whom they are trying to influence.'

In April 1961 he made a national issue of it, broadcasting an assault on 'party businessmen' and party corruption. 'Any member of parliament who wishes to be a businessman can do so, but he should give up his seat in parliament.' As things were, the rush for private gains was 'working to alienate the support of the masses and to bring the National Assembly into isolation'.

True words: but they did no more than tinker with the problem. The gap in living standards, between 'the top' of the C.P.P. and the majority of voters, was already wide and bitterly resented. Urban wages and cocoa farmers' incomes were lagging badly behind the cost of living. Meanwhile the men at the top were living in ease and comfort, and seemed firmly bent on getting more of both. Yet all Nkrumah felt able to say about this was that party members should own no more than two houses totalling a value of £20,000, no more than two motor cars, or plots of land worth more than £500.

This might seem to many a time to 'soak the rich' for the benefit of C.P.P. policies of social progress. Nkrumah's government decided to soak the poor. In July 1961 its advisers had their way. The government concluded that the country was living beyond its means, and a budget was brought in to meet the deficit. Nkrumah approved it.

What this sudden and savage budget did was to impose 'compulsory savings' so as to increase government revenue. All wage earners were to lose 5 per cent of their wages, deducted at source. All other types of 'assessible income' were to contribute 10 per cent, also taken at source. This included cocoa incomes, although cocoa farmers were already contributing about 13 per cent of the nominal price they were getting for their cocoa from the Marketing Board.

The effect might have been foreseen. It was one thing to say that expanding social services called for higher taxation. Schools and clinics undoubtedly cost money. But it was quite another thing to suppose that ordinary people would happily take a further cut in their standard of living, on top of recent falls in real wages, simply because they were getting more schools and clinics. They might have taken it, perhaps, if the budget had signalled an all-round cut in incomes, and if the C.P.P. had embarked on a rigorous campaign of honest explanation. Neither condition was fulfilled. All too clearly, the men at the top were going to escape deductions from 'assessible income'. As for the C.P.P., its machinery for persuasive explanation barely existed now.

The effect of the budget was not foreseen, and the Takoradi strike erupted. That proved another turning point.

Outraged by the 5 per cent levy on their wages, port and railway workers in this key ocean harbour struck against it. Their action was unofficial, because it had to be. Not only were strikes illegal, but the Trades Union Congress had become so closely identified with the C.P.P. that a single membership card was used for both; the Budget was C.P.P. and therefore T.U.C. policy. Yet the strike was solid, and it held for a long time. The strikers, commented *West Africa*, 'must be labouring under a very deep sense of grievance to have carried on for so long, in the face of so many difficulties, without any organization to assist them'.*

Yet the party of 'the plebeian masses', and its leader, had no time for this sense of grievance, however deep it might be. Returning from a conference of non-aligned nations in Belgrade, Jugoslavia, where he had found himself in his element, Nkrumah spoke of 'supposed grievances', a sharp reminder of his own failing grasp on the everyday reality of Ghana. It was true that a national minimum wage had been introduced a year earlier, and had done a little to offset the loss of workers' income by the inflation of these years. Yet a leader attuned to reality must have seen how little it had done.

In fact, the rise in wages had actually increased urban unemployment, a number of foreign-owned companies having discovered that their enterprises had become 'uneconomic', and closed them down. Far from being a 'supposed grievance', the general level of urban wages was probably lower, in real terms, even than in 1939. Independence had brought good things for the country as a whole, but the pockets of the poor were as empty as ever. Meanwhile the poor were abused for striking, while party bosses were told to own no more than two houses and two cars.

Not only did Nkrumah condemn the strikers; he also gave them an ultimatum: go back to work or be sacked. As it was, the police went to work and made arrests. The Preventive Detention Act was applied to no fewer than nineteen trade unionists in the Takoradi-Sekondi complex. As a popular party, the C.P.P. had declared war on itself.

Now at last Nkrumah saw the writing on the wall. There could be no clearer proof than the Takoradi strike of the general futility of trying to build a democratic prosperity on the basis

* *West Africa*, 23 September 1961.

of the kind of economic advice he had received, in floods, since 1951. All that could now happen, along those lines, was a continued widening of the gap between 'the top' and 'the base', and, with this, an ever deepening social strife. Independence must then become a mockery of the vision of a peaceful and progressive country.

The conclusion was not only his. It was also reached, for example, by the country's statistical office under the highly competent E. N. Omaboe. 'Despite the stupendous increase in output,' one of that office's official statements commented at about this time, 'the country is only running in order to stand still.' One may also note that some of Nkrumah's successors, after his overthrow, reverted to the same advice as Nkrumah had acted on but afterwards begun to reject. They launched another phase of 'growth', borrowing right and left to do so; and its futility then became terribly plain.

At this supremely difficult moment, Nkrumah once again showed that he could rise far above the level of a political boss concerned merely with hanging on to power. It would still have been easy for him merely to do that. He need only have abandoned any far-reaching aims, temporized with his difficulties, offered some rewards to his conservative opponents, and generally taken cover while the storm blew itself out.

He did none of these things. Though tardily, he drew some painful lessons from the Takoradi strike. There was now a choice, he concluded, between continued stagnation, 'running in order to stand still', and a rapid change of policy in a radical direction.

The choice was easy enough to make on paper, but very hard to carry through. If stagnation meant increasing strife, a 'turn towards socialism' called just as surely for men of socialist convictions. There were precious few upon the scene, while Nkrumah's own views on the subject remained extremely theoretical. In these unpromising circumstances he embarked upon the last large but least realistic enterprise of his life: he began to try to make a revolution, but without revolutionaries.

He looked around for candidates. One of those he found was

Tawia Adamafio, for long a journalist who had served the opposition. Adamafio now spoke like a radical, and Nkrumah made him the C.P.P.'s new secretary-general. How sound a radical Adamafio really was may perhaps be measured by his own reaction to the Takoradi strikers: he called them 'rats'. Yet Nkrumah's reaction had been no different. Like Adamafio, he seems to have seen no contradiction in pressing for radical change while hounding the unofficial leaders of the country's only solid group of urban workers. But he also found a more appropriate target.

ENTER THE ASSASSINS

He moved against this target, consisting of the new 'men of substance' of the C.P.P. government and its political machine, during a brief interval before enemies far more dangerous showed their hand.

Not a few of these 'men of substance' had found time, by now, to make themselves rather more than comfortable. They had acquired large houses which they filled with expensive furniture and *objets d'art* of a curious and wonderful vulgarity; and here they lived, amidst a host of lackeys, hangers-on and poor relations in an atmosphere of pomp and pretentiousness that might be quite disarming in its claim to show what the 'good life' should really be, but was also very offensive to a great many people.

Worse still, at any rate from the standpoint of their political reputations, they were anything but modest or discreet about their rise to wealth. For them, on the contrary, the great point about having wealth was to show that you had got it. In all these respects, of course, they were historically of the same mind and behaviour as countless other petty-bourgeois 'bene-ficiaries' of nationalist struggles and commercial enterprise in an earlier Europe. Their only peculiarity in the Africa of the early 1960s was that they were leaders in this, as also in worthier things.

Like other such persons before and after them, they were not in the least ashamed of their wealth, nor of the dubious ways, or even the downright dishonest ways, in which they got hold of it. Didn't their success prove how shrewd they were, and therefore how deserving of admiration? Wasn't it they, after all, who had borne the brunt of the fight for independence? And what was independence for, if it wasn't for their benefit? Those who cried out against them, they stoutly replied, were merely envious of opportunities which these critics, given the chance, would use in exactly the same way. Judged by what was going to happen after Nkrumah's overthrow, they were not so very wrong in thinking this. But meanwhile they handed weapons to Nkrumah's enemies.

Nkrumah began by imposing resignation on six leading members of his government, all veterans of the 'old guard' of 1949; among these were Komlo Gbedemah and Kojo Botsio. Others were told to surrender part of their property; among these was Krobo Edusei, who, perhaps a little unfairly, became notorious for the 'golden bed' which his wife, a keen business-woman in her own right, had lately added to her sense of comfort and prestige.

To these men Nkrumah's action seemed unfair to them, but also unwise for him. They felt they had nothing to reproach themselves with. All they had done was to behave as a 'growing middle-class' on the best pattern of foreign examples. If they had gathered in wealth by whatever means came to hand, so had all their forebears in every 'developing country' in the past, and not least in England and the United States. There was no other way for a 'growing middle-class' to grow. Besides, they had done their duty to the State, and, true to their own tradi-tions, they had taken care to provide for their relations. If highly respectable foreign companies were ready to pay them 10 per cent on contracts, who were they to reject such gifts?

Aware of their own worth, they retired to the sidelines, there to await another call to office; and it was not to be long in coming. Foreseeing trouble, most of them worked to reinforce their own inner-party positions. Gbedemah proved an exception. He preferred to go abroad. He had been perhaps the most effective of Nkrumah's aides in the past, and, as an active businessman and leading minister, had become a chief spokesman for 'continuity' and 'respectability'.

Now he made the break final and complete. In an 'open letter' to Nkrumah, he once again argued the case for 'continuity'; warned of the danger of offending foreign interests; and denounced the new policies as 'over-ambitious'. Entitled 'It will not be Work and Happiness for All!'—the C.P.P.'s new programme was entitled 'Work and Happiness'—this letter aimed some bitter shafts.

But they scarcely touched Nkrumah, who was now quite sure that 'continuity' could solve nothing, and who, in any case, had far more serious things to worry about. Fresh violence seemed imminent. Strange and threatening signs were now marked by the police, and not only by the police. Reacting to these in October 1961, the government announced that it

has become increasingly aware of the clandestine and dangerous activities of certain individuals in the country.

These activities are deliberately calculated to subvert and to endanger the security of the State. They include acts of violence, secret meetings, the taking of secret oaths to assassinate the President and certain members of the Government, strikes, sabotage and lock-outs. These are all designed to effect the violent overthrow of the legally constituted Government.

Mere alarmism? Save for the astonishing allusion to strikes that were very obviously a defence of wage-levels already painfully low, the evidence appeared to have weight. Apart from detaining the nineteen trade unionists, the police moved against thirty-one persons of another kind. Some of these, including Danquah, were no doubt innocent of any rebellious intention. But it soon became clear that rebellious intentions were on the scene.

As part of his African foreign policy, Nkrumah had succeeded a few months earlier in making a commercial agreement with

Ghana's northern neighbour, the newly-declared Volta Republic. This agreement was aimed at a customs union between the two countries; and, as part of it, Ghana had advanced £2 millions to Volta so as to compensate for customs dues in the meantime. The effort was later nullified by French banking interests who saw it as a weakening of the 'franc zone', and thus of French influence. But now it promised well, and was in line with other such initiatives of Nkrumah's government, such as a much larger loan to the Republic of Guinea a few years earlier.

To celebrate this small but useful step towards unity, Nkrumah arranged to meet the Volta president, Yaméogo, at the southern Volta town of Tenkodogo. The meeting took place on 31 July 1962. Returning to Ghana the next day, Nkrumah and his ministerial party made an unscheduled halt by the roadside. The place was called Kulungugu. A nearby 'bush school', it appeared, had sent a boy to offer the President a gift of flowers. So the cavalcade of cars made its halt, and Nkrumah was about to receive the flowers when a grenade was thrown. The boy was killed outright. Nkrumah was hit by small fragments in the back.

Beyond any question about the findings of judicial commissions, here was the 'riot and rebellion' prophesied by the N.L.M. in 1956. But whose hand was at work? The grenade thrower was not found, then or later; there was nothing to indicate his identity. But who in Nkrumah's entourage had arranged for a stop at the precise point where a man with a grenade was waiting behind a tree? It looked grimly like an 'inside job'. This is what the police and intelligence branch now said it was.

A month later they arrested Adamafio, the C.P.P.'s newly-appointed secretary-general, together with another well-known personality of the Ga ethnic group, Foreign Minister Ako Adjei, Nkrumah's old-time associate in the United States and England. These two, together with Coffie Crabbe, the C.P.P. executive secretary and supposedly another radical like Adamafio, were duly brought to trial. But not yet: the violence begun at Kulungugu first took an appalling toll in the capital itself.

Grenades were thrown in Accra, killing thirty people in the streets and wounding many others.

This time the police found solid evidence. Among those whom they arrested was an N.L.M. leader, Obetsebi Lamptey, lately returned secretly from neighbouring Togo: * evidence produced at the trial went to establish that he had supplied grenades and paid those who threw them. He and six others, similarly implicated, were found guilty by Chief Justice Sir Arku Korsah, sitting with Judges Van Lare and Akufo Addo. They were sentenced to death, but the sentences were at once commuted to imprisonment. Lamptey died in hospital soon afterwards of cancer of the liver.

Against this sinister and violent background, Adamafio and his two fellow-defendants were then tried for promoting the Kulungugu attempt on Nkrumah's life. There was no sound evidence. They were acquitted. But Nkrumah refused to accept this acquittal; and this was the next turning-point. Acting within the constitution, he caused the National Assembly to bring in an amending Act by which the acquittals could be declared null and void; they were so declared on 25 December. Then he went further. Still within the terms of the constitution, he dismissed the Chief Justice.

The dismissal was widely seen as a step without legal justification, and as widely criticized at home and abroad. What were Nkrumah's reasons for it? Immediately, it seems, he was angered by surprise. He had apparently been led to believe that the evidence against the three accused was conclusive, and must result in a verdict of guilty. Then, without warning, he found they were declared innocent. As the government's credit and his own credit were involved, he should have been informed beforehand; he should have been given an opportunity to prepare for an acquittal.

Behind this excuse, however, there lay probably a more

* One of the original 'big six' arrested by the British, and the same man who, with William Oforo Atta, had gone down to Saltpond so as to investigate Nkrumah's private papers for signs of 'communism'.

persuasive reason. Arku Korsah belonged to the 'old opposition' of the U.G.C.C., of the 'old establishment' who had continued to serve the State but without enthusiasm. The circumstances of the acquittal seem to have awakened Nkrumah's suspicions. Having broken with so many of his own 'old guard', he now proceeded to break with those remaining members of the Opposition's 'old guard' who still had leading State jobs. If new policies could alone save all that he had worked for, these policies no less clearly called for new men.

It was a fateful moment. After it, there could be no going back. But where was he to find these new men?

TOWARDS ISOLATION

A lack of courage and determination was not among his failings. Now he was going to need all that he had of both. Yet one has the impression, looking back on those days, that his confidence was repeatedly nourished by an unbroken faith in his own ability, as well as by his growing reputation up and down the world. Enemies in Ghana might try to drag him down, or sully his name with mud, or kill him. Outside Ghana he had nonetheless given the word Africa an entirely new meaning and respect. But what had these enemies in Ghana ever done except run to the British with angry tales against him and the independence he had won? He despised them thoroughly.

Though sorely beset by troubles, he still looked stubbornly ahead, searching for his way. Once again it proved a weakness of his character and formation that he even preferred to stand alone, deciding everything himself, the indispensable steersman on the bridge. It was possibly the worst frame of mind in which to persist in trying to make a revolution. But he persisted.

He had broken with the big men of the old establishment. He had ditched the old guard of the C.P.P. Almost at once he had come to believe that the leaders of his 'new guard', 'radicals' such as Adamafio, were unworthy of trust. This forced him to bring back some of the old guard; Ako Adjei, for example, was now replaced by Botsio as foreign minister. But these men took office as the instruments of his policy, and merely did what they were told. Before they had been his companions. Now they were only his employees.

Faced with a demand that it should lead a revolution, the C.P.P. was quite unable to respond. Asked to embrace non-capitalist policies, eventually socialist policies, its leaders were lost in disbelief or in confusion. Active political work among ordinary members had practically ceased, or else became a mere rubber-stamping of whatever headquarters might direct. And headquarters had become the government. Imperceptibly, the C.P.P. had ceased to be a political party. So little democracy did it have that its central committee was no longer elected; and the names of its members were not even allowed to be made public. Now it became a mere arm of government administration.

All this meant a deepening isolation for the man at the top. In some words of Michael Dei-Anang's, written long afterwards from much experience as one of Nkrumah's principal secretaries, Nkrumah was now led into 'a heavy reliance on the framework of the civil service and military organizations for the maintenance of his administration'. They it was, in practice, who were now asked to carry through a 'second revolution' that should bring social equality and social justice, and get the country on the move again.

The civil service did its job according to its lights, and the military were as yet, it seems, outside politics; but neither body was inspired by the least belief in socialist or any other radical convictions. This being so, the new policies of social change became identified with whatever Nkrumah personally said they were, or ordered to be done. So this 'second revolution' had to be one by bureaucratic order, a contradiction in terms and a crass separation of theory from practice.

How far did he realize this? It will remain hard to say, even when all the documents of that period eventually become available, in so far as they may survive. His was an often elusive personality, oscillating between a blind optimism and a shrewd calculation of the real possibilities, or between the empty slogans of revolution and a hard-headed grasp on the nature of the problems that faced him. Head and shoulders above all rivals on the scene, whether for courage or capacity, he still suffered from the unresolved confusions of his time and place. Highly intelligent, he could be intellectually shallow; ruthlessly clear on many things, he could be quite the reverse on others. It was a very human situation, with pettiness and grandeur marching hand-in-hand.

He enjoyed his isolation, but he also tried to work his way out of it. He launched an Ideological Institute at Winneba, a small town westward along the coast from Accra. This was designed to train party workers as socialists, though for the most part it did nothing of the kind. In December 1962 he founded a fortnightly journal, *The Spark*, named deliberately after Lenin's *Iskra* of revolutionary times in Russia long before. He welcomed the aid of non-Ghanaians who would help to form the Ghanaian revolutionaries without whom, as he certainly understood, he could not hope to succeed. One of these was a distinguished Nigerian exile, S. G. Ikoku. Others of communist persuasion came from England and elsewhere. Later he found a powerful publicist and constructive critic in a former radical senator from South Africa, H. M. Basner, whose articles in the *Ghana Times* were to be a fund of good sense and information. He took to lecturing himself. He tried hard to find responsive students who would enliven the C.P.P.

Yet none of this could do much good, or any good at all, in the absence of a political party capable of inspiring and accepting the participation of the mass of ordinary people. In this situation the radicals, even when they really were radicals and not political racketeers, could operate only as one more faction of a party leadership composed of warring cliques. They could write fiery articles in *The Spark*, but who except themselves would read these articles? And when at last the coup came, not even the 'trained revolutionaries' of Winneba were found upon the scene of battle.

By 1964, with these and other efforts at breaking from his isolation clearly of no real avail, there were many who began to think that the final act in the tragedy could not be far ahead. Like it or not, he had become the sole decider of what was done in terms of policy and government action. Was he therefore a dictator? He was anything but a dictator by intention, or in his general attitude to those who opposed him or tried to kill him, or in his political and social beliefs.

But he was terribly alone. He had to govern through a civil service or through party factions, playing off one against the other. Somewhere beyond this network of administrative intrigue there stood the people of the country, watching with indifference a political game in which they had no part. When the *coup* came, they too would be absent from the scene, just as they would continue to be absent from later upheavals of the same kind.

For the man himself, isolation seemed to strengthen his sense of purpose. He worked harder than ever, spread his activities ever more broadly across the scene, constantly took up new ideas and pressed them forward. Though the writing now almost shouted from its walls, he gave it little thought or preferred not to see it. Convinced of his own better judgement, he continued to wage his political struggles, whether at home or on the continental scene.

*

Here, too, one has the impression that a growing isolation seemed, to him, another proof of the rightness of his vision: the nearer he came to the aims of African unity, the stronger must the opposition be. Local and international interests would redouble their hostility. But that could give him no sound reason for turning back.

Long before many others, he saw that unity alone could overcome the economic and political weakness of Africa's new states. Now his sense of urgency far outstripped the times in which he lived. He began pressing for a complete African union.

'The African struggle for independence and unity must begin

with political union,' he had told the Ghana parliament as early as August 1960.

A loose confederation of economic co-operation is deceptively time-delaying. It is only a political union that will ensure a uniformity in our foreign policy, projecting the African personality and presenting Africa as a force important enough to be reckoned with.

I repeat, a loose economic co-operation means a screen behind which detractors, imperialists and colonialist protagonists and African puppet leaders hide, to operate and weaken the concept of any effort to realize African unity and independence.

But the tide was running fast the other way. In that same year of 1960, no fewer than sixteen colonies gained their political independence, at least in name and flag, and others would soon follow. For each of them, as for Ghana itself, this was an independence within colonial frontiers accepted as national frontiers. Each of these new nation states was fast producing its own élite of beneficiaries in power. Each of these élites was foreseeably preparing to enter upon what it saw as its rightful heritage. But even those who believed that Nkrumah was essentially right also thought that he was trying to go much too fast, and was out of touch with reality.

On paper he partly had his way. The charter of the Organization of African Unity, accepted in 1963, was deeply imprinted with his ideas. It provided for an annual assembly of heads of state, for an all-African council of foreign ministers, for a general secretariat, for a list of common aims and organs to which all members promised loyalty and membership. Yet this was a unity only of words, a unity only 'from the top down'. It reflected the Ghana situation on a continental scale. In Ghana there was no longer a party capable of unifying the people upwards from the base. In Africa as a whole there had never been such a party.

He pressed on, making the characteristic judgement that a good framework must in time produce a good content, instead of the other way round. Not surprisingly, his isolation now grew upon the African scene. Many resented him, if for a diversity of reasons. Some, like Julius Nyerere of Tanzania, chastised him for his interference. East Africa, Nyerere believed, could best contribute to continental unity by moving first towards regional unity. Although knowing little of East Africa, Nkrumah not only disagreed but actively interfered to obstruct the East African federation proposed by Nyerere to other East African leaders. It was one of Nkrumah's worst mistakes.

Others were hostile for other reasons. Among these were the more conservative leaders of the French-speaking states, closely under the jealous wing of Paris. Still others found his appointees dishonest, or his policies misguided. Among these were some of the leaders of the newly-emerged liberation movements in countries that were still colonies. They considered that he had failed to understand that a people which does not liberate itself cannot be liberated by any other people, at least in any worthwhile way. They saw this failure to understand their needs and aims in his projects for military intervention by independent states. Such intervention, even if it could have any practical effect, was the last thing they could want.

For many, too, the offensive ballyhoo of the Nkrumah cult had now become far more than they would take. It stuck most horribly in their throats. Even when they continued to respect and admire the man, they despised the adulation of his sycophants, and they blamed him for accepting it. The best of them found the cult insulting to their cause; but they also found it dangerous to him.

The truth of his position after 1963 is that he was increasingly a man besieged. It seems that he often saw it that way himself. Far from trying to broaden the 'power structure' in line with a genuinely radical policy, he continually narrowed it to himself, bringing more and more administrative business under his direct supervision. This was the time when the presidential compound of Flagstaff House saw the establishment there of 'secretariats' which doubled for the actual ministries, and gradually reduced the ministries to effective impotence. Yet the further he took this process, the further he had to continue it. The everyday political life of the country slowed almost to a standstill.

What should he have done to escape the consequences? Caught in the contradictions of his place and period, he could see no other way of moving forward, while going back would be tantamount to surrender, and he was not going to surrender. Faithful to the vision of his earlier years, he believed that he would be proved right. Perhaps because there was nothing else that he could believe and still hold on: let him only hold on, and all would yet be well.

ILLUSION AND REALITY

Much could be written about these last years. They were filled with incident and initiative of one kind or another. But the essential decisions were all taken. The final scenes of the drama were all prepared. The tragedy would run its course.

Before 1963 was quite at an end he announced his next step. Only the effort of heroic policies could unite the country on a new and popular basis, and enable it to break away from economic dependence and productive stagnation. These policies the country must approve. They would be asked to do so, symbolically, in a national referendum at the end of January 1964. Less symbolically, they would vote on two amendments to the constitution. One of these would enable the president to dismiss a high court judge 'at any time for reasons which appear to him sufficient'. The other, more important, would make Ghana into a one-party state.

There were some who did not wait to deliver their answer. On 2 January 1964, a police constable fired five shots at Nkrumah, missing him but killing a guard. Was this the eruption of another plot? If so, whose hand was behind it? The answers are still unclear today. After investigation the Commissioner of Police, E. R. T. Madjitey, was dismissed with eight other police officers, and afterwards detained. Preventive detention orders were issued against a police superintendent and some others, including Danquah once more. No culprits were found save the assassin himself.

Nkrumah took it coolly, as those who talked with him at that time can testify. I remember going to him to intercede on behalf of an American lecturer in law who, with several other foreigners, was now expelled in the wake of this new attempt at murder. He listened to what I said and pointed out that the police must have their reasons for the deportation. I argued that the police could also be mistaken, and that in this case they were mistaken. He looked at me somewhat wearily and warily, promised to consider the case, and nothing more was said upon the subject. But a little later the deportation order was cancelled.

Outwardly, at least, he stayed calm and his confidence appeared unshaken. There were those outside Ghana, among his serried ranks of critics, who said that he was now a frightened man, barricaded in his office behind tall screens of security. I am one of many who can affirm that this was simply not the case. It was easy to see him by appointment, if with some delay, and then it was easy to reach him through security checks that were little more than nominal. Once you reached him you found a man who was neither pretentious nor arrogant nor frightened, but much the same as he had been before.

This is not at all the picture suggested by the cult of his name and power. Yet the fact remains that he took this cult, even now, with more than a pinch of salt. In this, as well as in letting the cult expand, he appeared very much a man of his own country, sharing to the full in Ghanaian self-confidence and 'bounce', wit and zest for life, while believing, in a very Ghanaian way, in the sovereign virtues of the pursuit and management of power. He let the cult expand, and C.P.P. factions made sure that it expanded mightily: after all, they found it a useful screen for their own expansion. In all these ways the cult perhaps was also the product of a history old and not so old.

Fifty years earlier the Rev. Attoh Ahuma, distinguished local editor and author of *The Gold Coast Nation*, had deplored 'the evils incident to what is popularly known in Political Philosophy as One-Man Policy, and which obtains to a disastrous extent in West Africa generally, and on the Gold Coast particularly'. This One-Man Policy, he concluded, 'cannot be too much deplored. One-Man Policy, or One-Man Government, is indeed the curse of West Africa.' Nkrumah had always thought so too. His whole philosophy condemned it.

But he was trying to make a revolution without revolutionaries, and even his radical supporters went along with the cult. 'The charismatic personality of President Nkrumah,' declared *The Spark* in this period, 'is one of the props on which the new nation of Ghana is built. It is not one of mere personality worship. It is the most practical way of providing the new ship of state with a stable keel . . .' It was to provide one of the most practical ways of sinking the ship altogether.

With all this, the cult was nothing so extravagant as his enemies enjoyed saying that it was. His title of *Osagyefo* meant 'victor in war'. Some of his sycophants translated this as 'redeemer', and this translation was eagerly repeated by hostile newspapers as another proof of his madness. But nobody in Ghana thought it meant redeemer, and few would have cared if they had. *Osagyefo* was just another of Ghana's titles of tradition.

Nothing so portentous as the top-hatted protocol of Liberia ever took shape here, nothing so expensive as the palatial splendours of the Ivory Coast and some other such places. Even the tie-less working jacket adopted by Nkrumah, like the tie-less working shirt adopted by President Nyerere, was modest and a sensible adjustment to the climate.

Perhaps, too, a little splendour might have been forgiven. Accra had become an international centre of importance. Ghanaians had led Africa's entry to the councils of the world. Nkrumah's work had done much to sweep the old colonial epoch into the archives of history. He was proud of all this. If people praised him, he thought there were good reasons for it. If they attacked him, he thought their motives dishonest or misinformed; and he was not always wrong in thinking this.

He might have rested on his laurels. Not a few other African leaders were all too ready to rest on theirs. He might have accepted, as they were doing, a comfortable junior partnership in the corporation of international power that ran the world, or at any rate the African world. The attacks would then have quickly ended, and the 'bad boy' of yesterday would have become a welcome guest again. He knew all that perfectly well, and saw it as another confirmation of the rightness of his refusal.

Boxed in by circumstances and his own character, he embarked upon the minefields that now lay waiting for him. The referendum of January 1964 was the first of these.

*

The referendum gave him a huge majority: 2,773,920 votes in favour and 2,452 against. But such results do not come from an honestly conducted referendum. How improbable were these results could also be seen from the total poll that was claimed. This was 92·8 per cent of the registered electorate, a far higher proportion than had ever voted at general elections in times of widespread C.P.P. enthusiasm. Would an honest referendum have still given him a majority? My own opinion, for what it is worth, is that an honest referendum would still have yielded much the same result as general elections in the 1950s: a decisive but not overwhelming majority in a poll of about three-fifths of the electorate.

As it was, the C.P.P. became Ghana's only political party by the assistance of electoral fraud. And the reasons why this fraud occurred were the same reasons as would now ensure that the C.P.P. completed its own ruin, and, with it, Nkrumah's as well.

Party patronage had become a way of life. But patronage needs money, and the C.P.P. took it in handfuls from the only available source, which was the State. Just how much they took became clear only in 1966, when the new military rulers set out to find the answer. Among much else, they found a directive by which the Principal Secretary of the Ministry of Finance ordered the Cocoa Marketing Board to pay to the C.P.P. an annual subvention of £G400,000. Duly obedient, the directors of the Board had drafted a resolution to that effect: 'Be it resolved and it is hereby resolved by the Board,' ran this draft, 'that with effect from the 1st of January, 1965, the sum of £G400,000 be granted every year by the Board as a free grant to the Convention Peoples' Party.' In compliance with this directive, says the official document in which it was reported, 'subventions were paid to the C.P.P. up till the first quarter of 1966'. It was only one of many such arrangements, whether for personal or collective enrichment.*

But a system of party patronage on these lines led on to a system of personal patronage. According to evidence produced by the military rulers in 1966, Nkrumah similarly accumulated large personal assets, including some £454,000 in various Ghana banking accounts and £170,000 in Switzerland; it was also said that he had bought a handsome house in Cairo for his Egyptian wife, and owned some £8,000 in a London account.†

Written in a high tone of adjectival indignation, some of these accusations fail to convince, and others require factual substantiation; in particular, the assertion that he held large sums of money abroad appears to be without any substance. In discussing his morals in this matter, it is in any case relevant to ask what he did with such moneys. And it appears that the bulk of whatever moneys he thus abstracted from the State were not in the least applied to his own enrichment or comfort, but were especially applied to the furtherance of his anti-colonial and Pan-African purposes. They constituted a sort of 'secret vote' from which subsidies could be and were given to

* *Report of the Commission to Enquire into the Affairs of NADECO Limited*, not dated but late 1966. NADECO stood for National Development Corporation, one of the chief instruments of Nkrumah's new policy of state capitalism. For ancillary evidence, see also: *Summary of the Report of the Commission of Enquiry into Irregularities and Malpractices of the Grant of Import Licences*, 1967.

† *Report of the Commission (appointed under the Enquiry Act 1964) to enquire into the Kwame Nkrumah Properties:* submitted 12 October 1966.

other independence parties or groups opposed to colonial or neo-colonial regimes.

Other reasons can be found for a degeneration of the political system that was already, by 1963 or so, familiar in many other countries during this phase of primary decolonization. The Nigerian S. G. Ikoku, who knew the situation from the inside, has listed several of them.* One was the incapacity of the C.P.P. to unite theory with practice. This was not for lack of theorizing, at least on Nkrumah's part. He devoted a great personal effort to explaining the theory of possible social change in Ghana, and his books on the subject are a remarkable demonstration of this effort. But it was theorizing in a vacuum. It had little or no impact on the political machine.

Another weakness on Ikoku's well-informed list was the absence of any electoral process within the party's structure. Here the fault was very much Nkrumah's. Clashing with his theory, he had no trust in his party. He reserved the right to nominate all the members of the central committee, no doubt believing that in this way he could control the battle of the cliques. Perhaps: but the result was that party democracy entirely disappeared. All the way down the line to village level, decisions now came rigidly from above, and without discussion.

A third weakness lay in the fact that the party was identified after 1964 with the State, and so the State, as the stronger partner, wielded all the power, even if it did so in the name of the party. Thus it came about, as Ikoku explains, that it was the ministers of the government who dominated the mass organizations of the party, leaving these organizations without the least democratic energy of their own. They declined into being the mere puppets of the bureaucracy.

In all this his talents failed completely. Perhaps the basic reason lay in his formation during the years abroad: there he had shaped his vision in isolation both from political action and from the facts of colonial Africa. Afterwards, aloft on his pinnacle, he was never able to descend from it. Too much stood

* S. G. Ikoku, *Le Ghana de Nkrumah*, Maspéro, Paris, 1971, e.g., p .70.

G*

in his way: the nature of Ghana society and its product, the C.P.P.; his own failures of practical analysis; the speed and tumult of the times.

Again it is easy to be wise after the event. The early years of independence sowed many illusions; it was often difficult, then, to push through them to reality. Standing on his pinnacle, he came to see that Ghana must somehow escape from its 'inherited situation', whether political or economic. Everything that has since occurred in Ghana, or anywhere in Africa, has combined to show that he was right in this conclusion. But the means were simply not to hand, or he failed to find them.

His aims now were to diversify production, build light industries, lay foundations for a little carefully chosen heavy industry, reduce dependence on imported food, widen the whole working basis of the country. Convinced now that this should no longer be attempted by capitalist means, he looked for non-capitalist means. Other advisers came forward to provide the answers: there should be a vast extension of State enterprise, a turn towards co-operative production, a far more severe financial control of expenditure and commercial control of imports.

But this, like the policies of orthodox Western 'development', still supposed that an 'under-developed' country could become a 'developed' country by a reliance on foreign aid. It further supposed an active political campaign to ensure effective management of State enterprises, to launch and maintain new co-operatives, to guarantee a minimum of waste of public funds. No such campaign was possible. Waste and inefficiency grew in the same measure as expenditure.

The economic policies of 1964 and after were, in fact, another version of the old 'policy of growth' which argued that a mere adding to what already exists must in due course change what already exists. But countries without modern industry do not become industrialized countries merely by 'growing'. Far from that, the process has always demanded a more or less complete break with what 'already exists', just as during the industrial revolutions of England, France, or other technologically advanced countries. Nkrumah saw this too. But the practical means of bringing in the revolution that he preached were missing.

Merely adding to what already existed, in this situation, was only a way of piling frustration on confusion. There was the singular case of the Volta Dam and power development. An old project since the 1930s, this was carried through very success-fully by Nkrumah and his government. Potentially, the project was an admirable one. The waters of the Volta river were harnessed to provide cheap electrical power. This power, it was affirmed, would fuel new industries in Ghana. A new deep-water port was built at Tema at the same time, once again as a major contribution to the country's economic growth.

But what came of this growth? The Volta Dam certainly produced power for Ghana. Yet what it mainly did, in terms of development, was something quite different. One of Nkrumah's chief ideas was that Volta power should be used to process Ghana's bauxite ore for the eventual export of alumina and aluminium through the port of Tema. This required a smelting plant to transform bauxite into alumina, and a second plant to transform alumina into finished metal.

As it turned out, the smelter remained a promise. A plant to transform already smelted alumina was indeed built, but this alumina was not transformed from Ghana's ore. It was shipped into Ghana by an association of American interests from distant lands elsewhere. Ghana's cheap power, provided largely by the investment of Ghana's own capital, became a contribution to the development of distant people: and, according to Ghana's agreement with these foreign interests, the power was to remain cheap for a period fixed at thirty years. Ghana's bauxite remained where it was: under the soil.

The development of things, once again, came out as some-thing quite different from the development of people. One by one, as the end approached, his most cherished projects went the same way: they led to results that were exactly the reverse of those he had intended. The one-party state became a no-party state in any political sense that mattered. The new economic policies helped to fasten the country ever more fixedly into the 'inherited situation' of dependence on exports of cash crops and raw materials.

Even soaring cocoa production turned into loss. In 1964 the cocoa price began to fall steeply. In 1965 it collapsed to a near catastrophic level. And this was the moment when foreign debts incurred by the 'policy of growth', whether the old policy or the new policy, began to topple on his head. Then it was seen that far too many Ghanaian assets were mortgaged, by 'contractor-finance', to Western businessmen whose tenders were over-priced, whose terms of repayment were exorbitant, and who were often guilty of corruption. Then it was realized that not a few Eastern contracts, stipulating payment in sterling or dollars, worked in practice as devices for obtaining foreign currency for these countries at Ghana's expense.

The siege was nearly over.

TO THE BITTER END

Everything in those last months seemed afterwards to echo with foreboding. Rumour whispered more luxuriantly, but also more ominously. Meanwhile the drama dragged through its last scenes.

On 1 February 1966, the National Assembly gathered to hear the President's customary annual address. Wearing the buttoned-up jacket that he had introduced as a symbol of political renewal—somewhat modelled, it would seem, on the sartorial style of Chairman Mao—he offered a more than customarily sombre analysis of the situation. Like his jacket, the tone was anything but flamboyant.

He told them what was on his mind, and much of that, too, echoed with foreboding. 'All over our continent, we are beset by the forces of neo-colonialism.' Unless these forces were faced and overcome, the resultant disunity would 'spell chaos and confusion, *coups d'état* and boundary disputes, and be a breeding ground for corruption', as well as for 'conspiracies and intrigues'.

Armies might enter on the scene; but 'the substitution of a military regime or dictatorship is no solution to the neo-colonialist problem'.

Why was Ghana a one-party state? Because the mere imitation of Western parliamentary institutions could only engender 'chaos, confusion, corruption, nepotism and misery'. He might have added that the years after 1951, the years of compromise, had amply proved as much; indeed, he said this in different words:

The multi-party system which exists in Western countries is in fact a reflection of a social cleavage and the kind of class system which does not exist in African countries. A multi-party system introduced into Africa results in the perpetuation of feudalism, tribalism and regionalism, and an inordinate power struggle and rivalry.

But if that was obvious from all the evidence then to hand, something else was obvious as well. 'Let me emphasize that a one-party system of government is an effective and safe instrument only when it operates in a socialist society. In other words, it must be an expression of the will of the masses working for the ultimate good and welfare of the people as a whole.' Otherwise a one-party system 'can quickly develop into the most dangerous form of tyranny, despotism and oppression . . .'

The sentiments were above reproach, and the analysis a just one; but did the majority in Ghana any longer feel that the country's political system was 'an expression of the will of the masses'? Was it working, in their view, 'for the ultimate good and welfare of the people as a whole'? How far Nkrumah thought so, and was thus deceived, must remain an open question unless documents are found that can answer it. For he gave his confidence to very few persons now, and never publicly embarked upon the topic in his exile writings, save in a very general way. Addressing the Assembly, he was content to claim that: 'Here in Ghana, political power resides in the people, who make, enshrine and uphold our Constitution—the fundamental law of our land.' Events would soon add their own harsh comment.

He turned to the question of African unity, arguing once more that disunity among the newly-independent states would open the way for their individual failure. But 'united in a continental union government', these states could solve their problems, and ensure the 'potential for a new life'. He said much else along the same lines, and at a time when he was no longer alone in saying it. Yet the prospects of a union government for the continent were as remote as ever, and by all the signs seemed certain to remain so. Perhaps he should have said other things, less ambitious, more persuasive, much closer to reality; there is nothing to suggest that they could have made the slightest difference to what was now about to happen.

He listed Ghana's achievements:

Within the short span of eight years of independence, we have built some of the finest roads in the world; we have provided medical and health services for the large majority of our people; we have built universities, secondary schools, training colleges, and provided opportunities for free education for the great mass of the population.

And in saying all this he was not exaggerating much. Ghana had undoubtedly become a more comfortable and modern country. Not even his critics bothered to deny it, at least until their voices could alone be heard.

Ghana was still the victim of the world market, he continued: especially in the oversea price of cocoa, still disastrously falling. There was consequently a growing shortage of foreign exchange; at home, too much money was chasing too few goods. Inflation had become serious. They would have to cut down on a number of development projects.

Yet they could overcome these problems. New industries, he pointed out, were about to come into production. New men and women trained in scientific and other modern skills were about to become available. This expansion could and would continue.

As many as 400 new primary and middle schools had been opened in the previous year, pushing up enrolment by 200,000 pupils. Eleven new secondary schools had just brought the total of such schools to 101. There were three times as many students at the University of Ghana, not counting others at the new university at Kumasi, than four years earlier. New branches of administration included an institute of statistics; the Ghana medical school was about to begin its first year of clinical studies.

The great Volta Dam was at last completed, a year ahead of schedule. A smelter must now be made to follow. With all this, 'Ghana is now poised for a positive breakthrough in our agricultural and industrial revolution.' Considering the near-bankruptcy into which Ghana plunged during the second half of the 1960s, though not under Nkrumah's leadership, any such claim may appear absurd. Yet was he, looking back, so altogether wrong? Import controls were beginning to cut into the free-for-all havoc of foreign spending. Exchange controls were beginning to reduce the export of capital. Even allowing for all the confusion, mismanagement, corruption and anti-social hoarding of consumer goods that was now rife among traders speculating in inflation, one may still wonder what might not have happened if there had only been time: time for the cocoa price to rise again, time for the new policies to take a firm hold, and time for a more effective generation of managers and technicians to arrive upon the scene. Yet the fundamental problem would have still remained: the fact that the one-party state had become, in any real sense, a no-party state. And on that front, at least, there was not the least sign of any likely improvement.

There was in any case no time. Matters went rapidly from bad to worse. Food prices in the towns along the coast, especially the capital, soared beyond the reach of ordinary purses. This and much else was blamed on the C.P.P., and the C.P.P., reacting angrily to attacks on its political machine, further envenomed the scene. Scandals erupted. Expensive public projects such as a large conference hall were not stopped, and seemed to give a physical embodiment to the regime's apparent indifference to the plight of ordinary people. Gossip acquired a new edge of hostility.

Holding on, though now perhaps with an inner hopelessness, Nkrumah chose this moment to go abroad. Six months earlier, a Commonwealth prime ministers' conference had agreed to send a peace-making mission to capitals concerned with America's war in Vietnam, then beginning to plunge into its depths of mass destruction. No such mission had been sent. Nkrumah thought that he would go himself; perhaps he could do some good.

He flew from Accra on 21 February. It was the end of the road.

*

What would have happened if Nkrumah had not gone abroad? All that is obvious from the records is that many of Nkrumah's aides expected trouble as soon as his back was turned. Michael Dei-Anang has recorded, for example, that he and other officials were perturbed by the wording of a message from American President Lyndon B. Johnson. Nkrumah had sent Johnson a message some days beforehand, informing him of his own forthcoming visit to the Far East and to Hanoi, and asking Johnson to suspend the bombing of Hanoi for the period of the visit.

'Johnson's reply was terse, and lacking in enthusiasm, but it contained a memorable, and, what officials like myself in Flagstaff House considered to be ominous, passage: If you go to Hanoi, Mr President, you will be in no danger of American military action in Vietnam.' This struck Dei-Anang and his colleagues as an odd way of putting things; and there were more signs that appeared odd. 'Everyone had an eerie sense of things not being right somehow, and I was personally unhappy about something being "in the air" without being able to identify it specifically.'

Others also saw or sensed the signs of something in the air. 'Over the week-end of 18 February, Okoh [another of Nkrumah's senior aides at Flagstaff House] removed personal items from his desk; reports came in that officers were plotting a coup d'état in Kumasi.'* When Nkrumah left on the 21st, 'diplomats at the airport wondered if he would return'; and the American observer who wrote those words adds that he 'found several of these diplomats at the airport placing bets on the possibilities (and time) of a coup'.† It is even reported, by the same writer, that Nkrumah asked on the way to Cairo if the plane could turn back without landing, only to be told that it could not. He decided to go on.

*

The military *coup* followed three days later, resisted only by a small unit of Ghana troops garrisoned at Flagstaff House. The rebellious officers alleged that these troops included a number of Russians. No evidence that any Russian took part in the fighting was ever produced; and, as such evidence could scarcely have been overlooked if it had existed, and would, if produced, have powerfully fortified the military's case, one can safely assume that the Russian troops at Flagstaff House existed only in someone's imagination. In any case the resistance was soon overcome, and the rest of the country stood by with its hands in its pockets. There was some much-publicized rejoicing in Accra, always a centre of opposition, but otherwise there appears to have been no more public acclamation than would afterwards greet any subsequent change of Ghana's regime. The people, very clearly, no longer felt themselves involved.

*

Nkrumah was told of the *coup* while in Peking, awaiting the plane for Hanoi, and the moment must have been a terrible one. Soon, too, he found that all but a handful of his followers were fast running for cover. But he himself did not run for cover.

* W. Scott Thompson, *Ghana's Foreign Policy 1957–66*, Princeton, 1969, p. 412, quoting interviews with Ghanaian personalities.
   † ibid.

If he had been remotely like the monster of self-indulgence described by his enemies, duly possessed of great funds abroad, he would have retired to a villa in Switzerland, and there, no doubt, surrounded himself with the cohorts of concubines that he was also said to affect, while remaining content, like other dethroned potentates in similar situations, with the issue of an occasional blast of rhetoric against his enemies.

He did nothing of the kind. He went straight back to Africa. His old friend President Touré of Guinea welcomed him to Conakry, and clinched the welcome by appointing him to be co-President with himself. At once Nkrumah began broadcasting to Ghana, where the *coup*-makers responded with Draconic decrees of punishment for any person who should appear in any way regretful of Nkrumah's overthrow.

In Conakry he lived with his family in a small house within a garden, lying between a white wall and the sea; and here he went on with his work. In the years that followed he published many pamphlets and several short books, of which the most interesting from an historical standpoint was *Dark Days in Ghana*, where he made his preliminary analysis of the reasons for the coup which had overthrown him and his regime.

•

They were sad years, but it seems that he never lost heart, nor did he lack for friends. 'I had the privilege of knowing this exceptional man', the Guinea-Bissau leader, Amilcar Cabral, recalled after Nkrumah's death, adding that Nkrumah 'was a companion in our struggle who always knew how to encourage us in our hard fight against the particularly retrograde colonialism of Portugal'. Watching events in Ghana, moreover, Nkrumah saw his own predictions repeatedly confirmed: fresh attempts at progress by the 'policy of growth' that he had begun to reject in 1961, the policy of foreign spending and foreign borrowing so as to enlarge the *existing* system, led only to Ghana's still deeper failure and dependence. But there was nothing to show that he took any pleasure in the spectacle.

On 27 April 1972, at the age of sixty-three and six years after going to Conakry, he died in a Roumanian hospital where he was reportedly receiving treatment for cancer. Determined that his burial should be accompanied by the honour and respect that were due to such a man, President Touré asked for Nkrumah's corpse to be returned to Conakry. There he assembled a large gathering of African leaders so that they could speak about Nkrumah's life and work, and made ready to give him a state funeral.

But Ghana had changed in the meanwhile. Early in 1972, on 13 January, a group of officers led by Colonel Acheampong had quietly ousted the parliamentary regime of Dr Kofi Busia and his government, taken 1,301 officials of Dr Busia's Progress Party into custody,* and set about the mammoth task of clearing up the mess. Nkrumah was now remembered with a new warmth, and when he died there were strong demands that he should be laid to rest in his native land. Colonel Acheampong thought so too. 'I think he was a great man,' he said a little later.†

After lengthy negotiations, conducted partly by Nkrumah's old companion Kojo Botsio, it was agreed that Ghana would give Nkrumah's burial the honours for which Sékou Touré had reserved it. Botsio and Mrs Nkrumah accompanied the body to Accra. There it was laid in state.

Thousands of Ghanaians, led by Head of State Colonel Acheampong, filed silently past the body as it lay in state in Accra, while flags throughout Ghana flew at half mast and traditional drummers played outside State House, and Radio Ghana re-broadcast some of the ex-President's speeches and devoted special programmes to the former leader.

Members of the police and armed forces lined the route . . . as the body was borne on a gun-carriage for its 10-hour lying in state. After the lying-in-state the body was returned to the military hospital prior to burial in Dr Nkrumah's home-town of Nkroful. In

* *West Africa*, 8 January 1973, p. 52, at a moment when 215 still remained to be released.

† *West Africa*, 19 May 1972, p. 609.

Nkroful itself, local townspeople held an all-night vigil outside the home of Madame Nyaniba, mother of the late President.

Among messages sent on that occasion was one from Ghana's new leader. Colonel Acheampong's message said:

In his lifetime he waged a relentless war against colonialism and racism, and even after his death his spirit will, no doubt, continue to inspire the valiant fighters against these twin enemies of Africa. Today we mourn the loss of a great leader whose place in history is well assured. We join world leaders in paying tribute to this worthy son of Africa . . .*

* *West Africa*, 21 July 1972, p. 958.

Epilogue

A View for Tomorrow

He was the salt that seasoned Ghana and Africa.
His mother at his graveside

But if the salt have lost his saltness, wherewith
will ye season it? Have salt in yourselves, and have
peace one with another.

Mark ix, 50

Colonel Acheampong's graveside message went on to say, as
others at this time variously said, that 'like all of us, Dr
Nkrumah had his shortcomings. Perhaps the problems of Africa
and the world loomed so large in his horizon that he overlooked
certain serious difficulties and irregularities at home.' The fact
is very obvious in retrospect, and nothing can be gained by any
polemic about the size of Nkrumah's shortcomings.

His overall and lasting importance is not in doubt, and was
twofold. He led the way to political independence, and then
struggled with the still greater problems of making economic
progress. Much can be learned from his success, and much from
his failure. But because Africa (and not only Africa) still has to
struggle with the economic problems that did so much to bring
him down, more can now be learned from the failure than from
the success. And this is true for the same reason that gives
Nkrumah his overall and lasting importance: for he failed in
trying to reach the right goal, and not, like many of his time
and later, in trying to reach the wrong one.

Little can be learned about this failure from the immediate
circumstances of his overthrow. He himself asserted that foreign
intelligence services, and most of all the U.S. Central Intelligence
Agency (C.I.A.), had played a notable role in promoting the *coup*.
'Banners and posters, most of them prepared beforehand in the
U.S. Embassy,' he affirmed, 'were pushed into the hands of the

unwilling demonstrators.'* Others pointed to the same kind of evidence. 'United States Ambassador Franklin Williams in Accra,' recalled Geoffrey Bing, 'welcomed the military regime with the same enthusiasm as his colleague, Ambassador Claire Timberlake, had welcomed the overthrow' of Lumumba in the Congo.†

One would have to be very naïve to imagine that no such influences were upon the scene, though the actual manner and degree of their involvement remain obscure. After the *coup*, in any case, the Western powers hastened to express their happiness at the disappearance of a man whose government had begun, however erratically, to escape from the Western fold. But the crucial fact about the *coup* was that the vast majority of people appear to have made absolutely no objection to it. And this must be traced not to any great enthusiasm for the *coup*-makers, except in the ranks of the traditional opposition, but to the decay of the C.P.P. as a party of the people. This decay was so complete when the military struck that not even the C.P.P. machine itself responded with so much as a yelp. Even the party's most 'ideological' members were then found to have melted away like mist in the sun, though it is fair to add that quite a few of them were taken straight into prison.

The C.P.P.'s decay was at the centre of the stage. Could it have been averted? Did it begin because Nkrumah, building his party in the early years, chose the wrong men? The record suggests the contrary: in 1949 and after, more often than not, he worked with the men who could do the job that was there to be done; and, for the most part, they did this job and did it well. Did the decay then persist because he failed afterwards to replace the new 'men of substance' by others more penetrating in their analysis, or more devoted to the public good? It is easy to say so, and many have said it; but where and who were the men he should have chosen?

The truth is that the party was no longer able to produce

---

* Kwame Nkrumah, *Dark Days in Ghana*, London, 1968, p. 30.
† Geoffrey Bing, *Reap the Whirlwind*, London, 1968, p. 432: in this context its Chapter 12, like other chapters, is an able summary of evidence.

the leaders that he needed, for it was split by intrigue or personal careerism, and demoralized by its own bureaucratic attitudes to political work. No doubt there were exceptions; they were not many, and they were not enough. Beyond that, the truth is also that many competent civil servants served Nkrumah loyally and well; but if they were too honest to sabotage his policies, they were also too conservative to understand these policies, much less favour them.

Nkrumah's own personality and style of work can be seen to have done much to enlarge the decay of the C.P.P. Aside from such arguments, however, two less personal lines of criticism have occupied the centre of debate. The first of these is that Nkrumah should never have embarked upon his new policies of 1960 and after. If he had stayed content with the policies of 1957 and before, on this view all would have been well: Ghana would have gathered in the long-term fruits of political independence, and, advancing in step with Western policies and Western advice, would have been spared the miseries that set in after 1960.

This point of view is that of a large number of his critics. There is much to explain its vehemence. If Nkrumah fell without sorrow to the majority of the population, it was surely in some part because the majority of people were tired of the suffocating boredom and offence of rule by party hacks without talent or even, as it often seemed, good intentions. If many saw him go without lifting a finger of dissent, it was at least in part because the cult of his personality had become a painful excuse for bad government. If others did the same, it was also because the price of food had gone beyond their reach.

Yet it is a criticism, essentially, which ignores reality. Nkrumah changed course in 1960, or tried to change course, because things as they really were, and not things as he imagined them, demanded a change. Politically, the parliamentary system had failed to contain the hostility of the opposition. More and more, it was becoming—as in Nigeria a little later, as in other newly-independent countries then or soon—the vehicle for sectional, regional, or personal intrigue and conflict. This borrowed system could provide no sure guarantee of civil liberties, for it could not be safely operated without a Preventive Detention Act: no more here, as the bombings showed, than in other newly-independent countries. At the same time, it threatened to reduce the legislative process to a deadlock or a dogfight.

Perhaps a more skilful operator would have manoeuvred more skilfully, lessened conflict between this and that group, or more successfully played off one against another. Yet greater cunning or ruthlessness could not have solved the basic problem. This problem was that the multi-party state on Westminster lines simply would not work on those lines; and it would not work on those lines because the circumstances of Ghana were not at all the same as those of nineteenth- or twentieth-century Britain. If anyone should desire the proof of this, he need only consider how the Westminster system worked when re-installed by the Busia regime of 1969–72: regionalism, factionalism, and 'tribalism' became at once a major factor in affairs; and Busia increasingly was attacked as dictatorial.* Something quite different provides the central lesson of Nkrumah's fall: his *persistent* inability to correct the bureaucratic degeneration of the C.P.P.

A parallel lesson emerges in the economic field. If the level of urban wages and of average farming incomes was no higher in 1960 than in 1957, or even in 1937, this was due in no important sense to the usual reasons that have been advanced against Nkrumah's regime: to the inefficiency or recklessness

* No one has continued to say this as strongly as Ghanaians themselves. 'When he came to power in 1969, Busia claimed to be introducing Ghana to Western-style democracy. But what did we see?' wrote Mr Akwasi Bretuo of the Ashanti *Pioneer* in a letter to *West Africa,* 15 January 1973. 'Journalists in Ghana, like my humble self, who found it appropriate to caution Busia on his dictatorial tendencies, had to suffer. When I was to travel to the U.S.A. for further studies, the government had my international passport seized because I had attacked it in *The Pioneer,* the very newspaper which made Dr Busia what he later became.' Another correspondent disagreed with some of the points in Mr Bretuo's letter but agreed with his conclusion 'that Busia was dictatorial': letter of Mr B. K. Dogbe of Accra, *West Africa,* 19 February 1973.

of the C.P.P. leaders. Far from that, these leaders had listened to the most cautious and 'respectable' advice, and had regularly taken it. They had worked to uphold and prolong the basic economic structures and relationships of the period before independence. They had rigorously curbed inflation at the expense of working people. They had borrowed long and they had borrowed short. They had fully 'met their obligations' in the way of allowing foreigners to bring their capital into Ghana and take it out again as profits.

Yet none of this helped them. By 1960 or soon after it was clear, as Omaboe's statistical office duly reported, that the country was running only in order to stay in the same place. And the same place, as the Takoradi strike of 1961 so painfully showed, was a perfectly untenable place for any government vowed to the progress and welfare of the majority. Again, if anyone desires the proof, let him look at what happened when the Busia regime reverted to the economic policies of 1957. All that these policies were able to yield, at that more advanced stage, was a more advanced disaster. The country was still running, but now it was running backwards.

Nkrumah turned away from the policies of compromise because they did not work in any way that he could find acceptable; in 1972 the second military regime, that of Acheampong and his colleagues, was to turn away from the policies of compromise once again, and once again because they did not work in any way that men of conscience found acceptable. The reasons might be differently phrased; essentially, they were the same.

These reasons were better understood by 1972. If with varying clarity, it was now widely seen that no ex-colony could achieve a genuine and steady progress while remaining with the industrialized countries in the same overall relationship as before. This was a relationship which had helped the further development of the industrialized countries, whether directly imperialist or not, but at the price of impelling the ex-colonial countries into a downward spiral of relative but increasing 'under-development'.

And this increasing 'under-development' was primarily no

longer because of wealth transfer from 'poor' countries to 'rich' countries. Above all, by this time, it derived from the systematic weakness of the ex-colonial countries in their effective capacity to help themselves. Within this relationship, all real economic power of decision lay outside Ghana. The acceleration of capital accumulation in the 'rich' countries supposed the slowing down of such accumulation in the 'poor' countries. Nothing shows this more clearly than the helpless posture into which Ghana eventually fell. It was part of Nkrumah's clarity that he understood these things, and their probable consequences, earlier than most other people, even if he found that he could do little about them. His detailed arguments were set forth in a number of his writings, notably in his book on neo-colonialism.

A second major criticism has come from another direction, this time almost entirely from outside Africa. According to this line of thought, Nkrumah should never have made the compromise of 1951, should never have 'bought the British plan', but, on the contrary, stood out for revolutionary demands from the very start. By accepting the reformist concessions offered by the British, on this view he fell into a British trap that was bound to prove fatal.

This second criticism is similarly subjective, as I hope this book may have helped to show. It is a criticism that has almost no connection with the reality of the situations in which Nkrumah and his fellow-leaders of the C.P.P. had to operate. It grossly under-rates the historical achievement of 1951, just as it under-rates the further achievement of 1957. Aside from that, one must repeat that neither in 1951 nor in 1957 was there any 'party of revolution' on the scene, nor even any significantly sized groups of that mind; and the most important reason for this absence was that there was also no revolutionary situation on the scene. So little was there a revolutionary situation on the scene that the C.P.P., once in office, was never able to mobilize a majority of the total electorate, and no more than three-fifths of the actual voters.

It is impossible to understand the complexities of the struggle for liberation from a standpoint of *a priori* dogmatism or theoretical complacency. The struggle for liberation has to be understood for what experience has amply shown it to be: a difficult choice between possible alternatives, none of which can offer a 'pure' gain, but only, at the best, a greater gain than loss. The alternatives that Nkrumah chose, whether in 1951 or 1957, offered much loss; but it will be hard to think they did not yield a still greater gain. They yielded this for Ghana, but they also yielded it for colonial Africa as a whole.

In the case of the liberation movements in the Portuguese colonies, for example, it may certainly be shown that they have been able to forge powerfully democratic movements of mass participation, precisely because they have accepted no demoralizing policies of compromise. But the historical fact is that they took the road of revolutionary change only after it became clear that there was no road, for them, of reformist change. The only 'Portuguese plan' that they could 'buy' was a plan for their continued and complete subjection. Yet the pioneers of these movements had nonetheless thought that 'the idea of autonomy'—of the Ghana compromise of 1951—was 'the only realistic step forward'. And, in the words of one of them, 'it was the independence of Ghana, and afterwards of Guinea [1958], that opened the view upon a different road.'* Then Portuguese intransigence helped to do the rest.

To argue from this that it would have been 'better' if the British had not been pressed to withdraw by compromise, but forced into the same stay-put-at-all-costs attitude as the Portuguese, is to misunderstand the necessary nature of the political process. Men act as they can, and as they believe they should, according to their circumstances. It is also to argue in a vacuum, for this is simply not what happened or could happen. Further, it is to overlook the appalling human cost of armed resistance against modern weapons of mass destruction.

The great achievement of the liberation movements in the

* Vasco Cabral, a veteran leader of the P.A.I.G.C. (Guinea–Bissau), in conversation with the author, November 1972.

Portuguese colonies is to have known how to make progress against a 'particularly retrograde colonialism', in Amilcar Cabral's definition. But this progress has been made far less by military action than by promoting real gains for liberated people in their daily lives: gains that are felt to be far greater than the loss caused by Portuguese bombing and burning. Similarly, the great achievement of Nkrumah and the C.P.P., in the period of primary decolonization, was to win real gains for the people of Ghana at a cost that did not cancel them out, but only reduced them. They are different achievements in different periods and situations; but they go in the same direction.

On a more personal level, could Nkrumah have done better than he did, after 1960? Essentially, the answer depends on how well or ill one thinks that he was doing by 1965, when the cocoa price collapsed. In certain important ways, as these pages have sought to explain, he was doing very ill. Yet it remains more than possible to argue that the basic policies then in play, even allowing for their inefficiencies of application, would have averted the near-bankruptcy of 1971, and, with a recovery of the cocoa price, would have launched a period of genuine and therefore durable expansion when inefficiencies could have been reduced.

It is quite impossible, on the other hand, to argue that the policies of the Busia regime (1969–72) could have ended in anything but the disaster which they duly encountered. Such was the debt position even by 1971—thanks to short-term borrowing on a scale that put all previous records in the shade— that the Busia government was about to ask for a 100 per cent moratorium on all its debts, short or long, for at least ten years, something that Nkrumah's government had never had to contemplate. And this was accompanied by a sycophancy and self-abasement towards foreign lenders which Nkrumah's Ghana had never known, and which mocked the claim to a reinforced independence that the Busia government made.

So far did this sycophancy go that the Busia government's high commissioner in London, addressing the Royal African

Society in London in June 1971, even tried to show that the regime was 'a bulwark against communism' on the grounds that 'there was now a fully recognized opposition whose leader was paid two-thirds of the prime minister's salary, besides being provided with a car and a chauffeur'.* Were the members of the Royal African Society supposed to conclude that the leader of the opposition was 'safe from communism' so long as he didn't have to walk to work or drive his own car?

Beyond the limits of this kind of argument, which is not worth carrying further, it appears that Nkrumah's long-term aims—socialism at home, unity in Africa—could for a long time have met with no more success than in 1965. This is not to say that his policies might not eventually have launched a genuine expansion, and thus laid the foundations for further advances at a later period of development. Nor is it to say, of course, that Nkrumah's aims were a mis-reading of the needs of the future. But what is right is not necessarily what is possible at once: what is right, in this kind of thing, is likely to become possible only by a step-by-step advance towards it. At least after 1962, Nkrumah wanted to go too far too fast.

His trouble was that he saw the future far more clearly than he understood the present, not an altogether rare case among prophets. His ideas about black unity formed in the distant and different conditions of the United States; his impatience to have 'all his tomorrows today'; his under-rating of the crucial importance of the decay of democracy inside the C.P.P.; his tendency to accept the slogans of mass participation for the thing itself: all these helped to separate him from the possible route towards socialism and unity, from all that slow and long but necessary work of building a revolutionary party securely from the ground, and in such a way that its roots stay firmly nourished in the soil of mass participation.

His central problem came from the fact of being involved in a contradiction between what was practicable and what was

* Quoted in *African Affairs*, Journal of the Royal African Society, London, vol. 71, no. 282, January 1972, p. 84.

desirable. History has peopled its pages with heroic figures who have played out the drama of their lives in that situation: with heroes who have followed their star no matter what the cost, whether to themselves or to others not in the heroic business. Writing over a century ago, Engels drew attention to the case of Thomas Münzer, the revolutionary leader of the German peasant wars at the beginning of the sixteenth century. It is one that bears consideration even today, and perhaps especially in peasant Africa. Münzer wanted not only to lead the peasants in despoiling the wealth of Germany's feudal princes; much more, he wanted to overthrow their power and lead the peasants into an entirely new society where there would be 'community of all possessions, universal and equal labour duty, and the abolition of all authority'. Having failed, Münzer was stretched upon the rack and then beheaded.

Engels's commentary has its application to Nkrumah, even though the terms need revision. 'The worst thing that can befall a leader of an extreme party,' commented Engels, 'is to be compelled to take over the government in an epoch when the movement is not yet ripe for the domination of the class he represents, and for the realization of the measures which that domination would imply.' What he *can* do depends not upon himself but upon the socio-economic stage of development in which he has to work; what he *ought* to do, according to his own understanding and conviction, cannot be achieved. He is compelled to act within the present while acting as though the present were the future. 'Whoever puts himself in this awkward position is irrevocably lost.'

Münzer's case was obviously far more extreme than Nkrumah's. 'Not only the movement of [Münzer's] time,' Engels continued, 'but the whole century was not ripe for the realization of the ideas for which he himself had only begun to grope.' Nkrumah's ideas were much closer to reality. Yet the parallel is instructive, and the outcome was of the same order. 'The social transformation that [Münzer] pictured in his fantasy was so little grounded in the then existing economic conditions that the latter were a preparation for a social system diametrically opposed to that of which he dreamed.'* In a much narrower and more temporary sense, Nkrumah's regime can be said to have paved the way for another regime, though not for a social system in any stable meaning of the term, whose ideas were diametrically opposed to its own. The difference, of course, is that we live in a time when policies aimed at socialism and unity can alone solve Africa's problems, so that all alternatives can be no more than temporary diversions from the pathway to those aims.

Nkrumah's life can to this extent be seen as a tragedy, and to this extent it was one. Served by a political machine which lacked the capacity and structure, and often the will, to realize his aims; deserted in the end by nearly all his old companions; spattered with every kind of mud by all and sundry, he was thrust aside and left to die. Yet it seems unlikely that history will see him as a tragic figure. In the degree that history will consider his failure less important than his success, his weaknesses less significant than his strengths, and all the weary flim-flam of his cult as counting little against the solid substance of his influence upon events, Nkrumah will be seen, to repeat Cabral's words, as 'the strategist of genius in the struggle against classical colonialism'.†

The view for tomorrow is therefore that Nkrumah's aims were the right ones, and that their realization will become increasingly possible as conditions ripen, and as other strategists take up the further struggle for liberation. These strategists will succeed in the measure that circumstances, as well as their insight and courage, enable them to do what Nkrumah did not do or could not do: in the measure that they undertake and carry through the work of building democratic organizations which become the vehicles of mass participation as well as of mass support: movements in which the mass of ordinary people really 'make,

* Friedrich Engels, *The Peasant War in Germany*, London, 1927, pp. 135–6.
† Amilcar Cabral, 'Allocution au Symposium organisé par le Parti Démocratique de Guinée, Conakry, à l'occasion de la Journée Kwamé Nkrumah, le 13 mai 1972': my translation.

enshrine and uphold the fundamental law of the land'. Then the confusions and the miseries of this intermediate period, the period of painful preparation and continual strife, will at last begin to give way to a new society, nationally and internationally, that can bring both peace and progress.

But the view for tomorrow also reflects Nkrumah's work during the 1950s, the period of his main achievement. Perhaps a last word here should be left with a Ghanaian. It is that of one of Ghana's most experienced administrators, A. L. Adu, a man well placed by his work to have known the inside story. Summing up for an American investigator in 1967, he said:

Ghana succeeded in making the impact of African diplomacy felt in international forums and international organizations. Ghana succeeded in mobilizing Africa's efforts towards the emancipation of the dependent territories.

Ghana succeeded against formidable obstacles of inertia and opposition in making the idea and ideals of African unity accepted all over Africa as the ultimate objective for all African states, whatever disagreements there might be on the ways and means of achieving this objective.

Ghana succeeded in making Africans everywhere feel proud of their Africanness and in a real sense in galvanizing the spirit of 'African personality' in international organizations. Most of these successes are due to the sense of dedication, of purpose, of single-mindedness, and the inspired leadership of Dr Nkrumah.[*]

It is a proud claim, but few other Africans have felt disposed to question it. For Nkrumah's Ghana put the world to school about the reality of Africa and the humanity of black people. Much of the world disliked the experience, or refused to attend, or preferred to play truant. But much of the world did not; and the much that did not was set upon the task of re-thinking its basic attitudes towards the history of Africa and the inherent equality of Africans among other peoples. With all its implications for the common good, this may be his proper epitaph.

[*] In a communication to W. Scott Thompson of 15 July, 1967, quoted in Thompson's *Ghana's Foreign Policy*, Princeton, 1969, p. 414.

Index

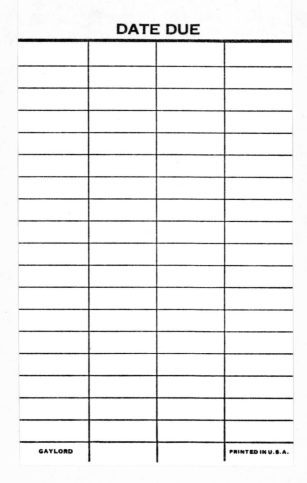